Achieving Results
through Time Management

Achieving Results through Time Management

Philip E. Atkinson

PITMAN PUBLISHING
128 Long Acre London WC2E 9AN

© Philip E. Atkinson 1988

First published in Great Britain 1988

British Library Cataloguing in Publication Data

Atkinson, Philip E.
  Achieving results through time
  management.
  1. Executives——Time management
  I. Title
  658.4'093   HD38.2
  ISBN 0-273-02733-6

Set in 10/13 Palatino by ⚑ Tek Art Ltd, Croydon
Printed in Great Britain at The Bath Press, Avon

To Ann, Sarah and Jonathan

Contents

Preface

This book should change the way you think about how *you* spend your *time* and how you live your *life*. This book has been written for the practising manager, the self-starter, the high achiever who is keen and enthusiastic to achieve results through time management.

It does not matter what your job is, or the level you occupy in the hierarchy. The status you hold and the type of work you do is unimportant. What is important is that you *can* achieve more in your time at work. All you need to do is to apply some of the principles which are outlined in the text.

Hopefully, most of the book will reflect your needs. However, the constraints and the demands of your work will determine which sections of the text are particularly relevant to you.

Approach this book in a flexible manner. Aim not just to read it, but to *use* and *apply* the major points to your work situation. The application of some of the basic principles will radically improve your performance. Changes in your behaviour will create the 'domino effect' whereby you will be able to influence the actions and behaviours of others.

Part 1 deals with examining the major problems with *time mismanagement*. Within this section, the 'methodology' or 'action framework' is developed to help you find out where the time goes, and then plan new techniques to get more out of the working day.

Part 2 focuses upon strategies to create new, more effective personal skills to achieve results and become more successful.

Part 1

Assessing time mismanagement

Chapter 1

Time. Don't waste it!

Why did you buy this book? Well, it's pretty obvious you think you can get more out of your day, and of course you can. You see, there aren't too many secrets behind effective time management. The principles are no more than common sense.

But if they are just common sense why haven't we all become effective at managing our time? Quite simply we do not devote sufficient time and energy to planning this most precious resource of all.

Next time you are at the office look around you. How many of the people you work with have developed good time management habits? Unfortunately you might find very few. But let's have a look in more detail. When you can find the chap who manages his time well, think about what separates him from his work fellows.

No, he isn't obsessive about always making lists. No, he doesn't rush around all the time with paper in his hands. And he probably spends little time worrying about his job. But what does he do? Well, he is one of those rare breed of individuals who sets *priorities* and actually does something about achieving them.

Do many managers manage their time well? I'm afraid not. Evidence from workshop sessions suggests that the vast majority of managers can get much more out of the eight-hour day. How often do I hear, 'If only I had more time'. This is the voice of regret and despair. Some managers actually believe that if they had twenty-eight hours in the day they would do more, and they would not be time pressured. It doesn't work like that. They still would be pressured because they don't really understand the 'working smarter' principle. It's not the time in minutes and hours you work, it's *how* you work and how you *structure* your available time which determines your rate of *success*.

To illustrate this point I can recall the best piece of advice I received from a management tutor when I was a student:

**'You don't have to work harder,
you only have to work smarter.'**

Of course he was right. But how many of us follow that precept? Very few. In fact, some people work against themselves. They refuse to believe they can work smarter. How often have you watched the budding young manager staying late at the office. Probably too often. He is suffering from the old 'myth' of believing that being seen to be working is the same as actually achieving something. Like too many managers, he can't differentiate between simply being at work and actually doing it!

Well, what can we actually do? How can we get more out of the day? And how can we ensure we do something of value *every* day?

First of all we have to get rid of this silly notion that we don't have enough time. We have plenty of time, we just don't use it wisely. This can be illustrated by stating Parkinson's Law.

'Work expands to fill the time available for its completion.'

Every day we start the day with the same time as everybody else. But where does it go? Unfortunately we waste time by neglecting to think about priorities. We allow our likes and dislikes to obscure our vision, cloud our judgement and regulate the day. As soon as this happens our preference, rather than the demands of the job, dictates our performance.

So what can we do to improve our performance? Read on. The secrets of achieving results are in the following chapters.

What is time?

Time is the most valuable resource we have at our disposal. We can't store time in a bank, nor can we buy time. All we can do is use it constructively or waste it. Time is a managerial asset which is irreplaceable and should be treated as such. Time is a scarce resource and the ultimate managerial constraint.

In *The Effective Executive* Peter Drucker maintains that time management is one of the key attributes of the effective executive. He states, 'effective executives know that time is the limiting factor.' Although many managers are sold on the 'time is money' theme, I still hear these comments coming from experienced managers.

'Why is time management so important?

'Surely we should be spending time learning to relax rather than learning how to use our time?'

These are the typical questions asked by managers who attend time management workshops. At the end of a two-day session, their attitude has changed drastically. They have learnt to value time and consequently feel more at ease and, at last, are more able to achieve results.

To illustrate this point consider how much time we have at our disposal. There are only twenty-four hours in the day. Generally we spend eight hours sleeping, allocate eight hours for work and spend the rest travelling, eating and relaxing. If we don't make the most of the eight hours at work, we can end up either staying late or taking work home with us. Sometimes we end up doing both. In effect this reduces the amount of time we have to spend relaxing, with our family or pursuing our interests or hobbies. The major point here is: 'If we can't make the hours work for us, we end up spending less time doing the things we enjoy.'

Relaxation is an essential component of the managerial day. Constantly working and spending our time doing work which has little payoff leads to frustration, anxiety, conflict and stress. An effective manager is a healthy manager, who develops a sense of balance and uses his time in the best possible way. He constantly asks himself, 'Am I making the best possible use of my time right now?'

Developing this point, many managers find that after they have analysed 'how they use their time', they then make a definite commitment to planning time for relaxing. However, at first many managers portray the characteristics of Jim, our fictional manager who, for some reason, is well known to workshop members!

Let's look at a day in the life of Jim, a middle-aged manager. Jim arrives at work at 0910, greets his secretary and settles down to his first coffee of the day. He has a rough idea of the work he has to complete, but decides to deal first with the morning mail. Gill, his secretary, brings in the mail and Jim wades through it. Unfortunately, most of the 'in' tray is occupied by sales brochures from suppliers, reports marked 'for information only' and a few memos requesting information.

Unfortunately, one of the brochures sports a scantily dressed young lady. The marketing boys win again! Jim's attention and his time have been diverted. Jim reads through the information, takes another admiring glance and eventually gets down to thinking about the memos.

Too late, Jim. The phone rings, and he deals with a routine enquiry. Coffee-break comes and goes and he turns his thoughts to the progress meeting in the afternoon. He thinks he has plenty of time to prepare for it, so 'why not leave it till after lunch?'

Arriving late back from lunch, Jim is summoned to the MD's office.

The meeting is being brought forward and the MD wants to be sure that progress is up to date.

You lose again Jim!

He has made the classic mistake; he has let routine, careless habits ruin his day, his image with the MD and possibly his career.

Do we make the same mistakes? Of course we do. Somehow we squander our time without realizing it. We give little thought to time. It is frittered away. Sooner or later the dreadful reality that time is passing hits us, often too late.

The time we waste is *important*. Consider this statement:

'We spend too much time at work.'

I think most people would agree. If we planned our day and made it work *for* us, instead of *against* us, we could be proud of our achievements. We may even be respected by our colleagues as an organized manager. More importantly, we wouldn't have to stay late at the office, taking home heavy briefcases and then feeling guilty about not being with the family.

The negative cycle of 'poor time management' strikes again. Poor planning and the resultant time-wasting means we have to stay late at work or take work home. If this is allowed to continue, it can lead to anxiety, the fear of not meeting deadlines, and a feeling of guilt because we do not spend time with our partner and children, etc. No one wins. So when are we going to change the situation and take responsibility for what happens to us?

It starts now. Read on.

Attitude

The biggest stumbling-block to developing new, more innovative and time saving habits, is *attitude*. This alone stands in the way and can stop learning.

Be prepared to unlearn old ways and habits. Commit yourself now to the culture and philosophy of the book. Experiment with the book, scan through the following chapters.

If you have remained with me this far you are on the way to changing your life, but one last indulgence. Sit back and waste some time for the last time.

Go on, waste it! But there again you could read on!

Chapter 2

Where does the time go?

Work is a central life interest for most managers, but we all need time to relax from the stresses and strains of business life. Time management helps us do just this. The effective time manager who gets at least ten hours out of the normal working day does this by working with purpose rather than just working harder.

The successful manager follows Drucker's advice and distinguishes between efficiency and effectiveness:

'Efficiency is doing the job right, effectiveness is doing the right job.'

I am sure that we all know people who are 'efficient'. They are always busy and achieve very little. The 'effective' manager ensures that he commits his time to achieving *high priority, key results.*

Time management is the key to *effective management.* Following time management principles, and applying them to your special circumstances, will help you achieve more. It will also enable you to create the domino effect amongst those with whom you work, including your staff, your colleagues and your boss. Your new habits and *effectiveness* will impact upon and influence their actions and behaviour.

How well do you manage your time?

Many managers believe that they use their time in the best way possible. Managers also feel that assessing and recording where time goes is an encroachment on their world. Many perceive new techniques as a threat, rather than as a means to achieve more and reduce stress.

Some managers believe that their position is sufficient to reflect their ability and authority to manage. They know how to do their job! After all, that's what they are paid to do. But, if quizzed, many would agree that if they had two more hours in the day, they could achieve more.

Well, we can't design a day with twenty-six hours, but we can help you to make the most of your time. *How*? Look at the following list of the symptoms of poor time management. How many of these are applicable to you?

Symptoms of poor time management
- Never having time to do the really important work.
- Devoting too much time to the 'urgent' rather than the 'important'.
- Frequently staying late at the office.
- Taking work home.
- Rarely having time to keep up to date with the paperwork.
- Doing the work of others.
- Feeling indispensable.
- Attending too many meetings.
- Having difficulty in saying 'no'.
- Letting others dictate how you use your time.
- Frequently feeling stressed, anxious and time pressured.
- Rarely completing work on time.

If you experience more than fifty per cent of these symptoms you are needlessly over-stressed and can *learn* to work more effectively.

When managers realize they are the *victims* of time mismanagement, they can then create change. They can take action and make time work for them.

We all have a life store of time. We should plan to make the most of it. Time is a scarce resource. Yesterday is gone. Let's make the most of tomorrow.

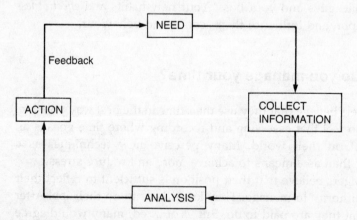

Fig. 2.1 Systematic approach to time management

To get the most out of this book we need to develop a systematic approach to time management. There are four stages to this approach (see Fig. 2.1).

The need for time management

First, managers have to recognize that a *need* exists, i.e. you have to be committed to examining new methods for getting the most out of the day. Without commitment and *motivation* you will not succeed. If managers fail to recognize that they could, should, and can, get more out of the same time, they will never be able to unlearn old habits, and develop new, more effective behaviours.

Once the need is established you have to find out where time goes. Who uses it? How much time do you spend in meetings? On the phone?

The only way to find out is to *collect information*. Most managers keep some form of diary. This helps to regulate the working day and plan the use of time. We are going to ask you to keep a *time log* (see Fig. 2.2). You have to account for your time. Keep the log for ten days and fill it in twice a day. To use the log decide on a time period (half-hour segments conveniently split the day up). Then log for each segment what you did. Who took up the time? And what was the outcome?

Time period	What happened	Who was involved	What was the outcome
0900–0930			
0930–1000			
1000–1030			
1030–1100			
1100–1130			
1530–1600			
1600–1630			
1630–1700			
1700–1730			
1730–1800			

Fig. 2.2 Time log

There are some major points which have to be developed before using the log. First, filling in the log may appear time-consuming, tedious and boring. It can be! But it is a small price to pay for accurately finding where the time goes!

Many managers believe that they really do control their time. They also believe that they know where it has gone. Unfortunately, the manager's self-perception of his own role, performance criteria, and key results areas can be distorted. His clarity of vision is blurred and he sees only what he wishes to see. Consequently, the disparity between perceived and real consumption of time is high.

Collection of effective pertinent information is the key to time management behaviour. If managers are unwilling, or not disciplined, to fill in the log, then clearly their perceived need to improve their performance is low.

Many participants in time management workshops state how difficult it is to discipline oneself to use the log effectively. But those who have done so recognize very quickly all the trivial events which happen each day. These trivia eat into their time, keep them late at the office and act as unnecessary stressors.

Once a group of managers becomes committed to using the log, information is recorded accurately. The next phase is sharing of information, where managers trust each other sufficiently to expose their bad habits to their colleagues.

Support groups

It really works well if you can get a small number of colleagues to work together. This ensures that everyone is disciplined and committed to looking at those things which do not just influence or reduce the effectiveness of you as a manager, but of the group as a whole. The group approach gives you the opportunity of getting rid of those things which impact upon you and others, those organizational issues which may appear trivial but which really restrict and limit your ability to achieve the goals you seek.

Trends and patterns

After ten days, trends and patterns appear. So let us move on to the next stage.

Time analysis

The third stage is *analysis*. This requires you to find out what consumes your time. Once you have a list you will have to distinguish between the *legitimate* time users, those things and activities which lead to personal and organizational success, and the *time wasters* which create little of value to you and the organization.

Once you identify the prime time wasters you can develop strategies and tactics to get rid of them once and for all. Just think how much more effective you would be if you managed to eradicate the principal time wasters in your life and your job.

Action plan

The final stage is *action*, where managers devise new innovative ways of structuring their time and their day. This means that they have to develop a plan that is structured around real priorities. The plan is a blueprint for ensuring that they fulfil the targets in their *key result areas*.

If you have been disciplined, have followed the key activities and taken the appropriate action, you will have eradicated the need to improve your use of time. But be careful, you can soon slip back into old habits. I find it useful to go through this exercise at least once every six months. There are always new time wasters waiting to consume your time and reduce your effectiveness!

Now it's over to *you*.

Chapter 3

Identifying the time wasters

Many managers assume that they can give a precise breakdown of how they spend their day. They feel that they have control and know how to get the most from their time. But, if you can keep a log for a period of two or three weeks you will be surprised what you spend your time doing! Many are sufficiently arrogant to tell you that they can identify where their time goes, and that they know how they use their day.

Some time ago a good friend told me he had nothing to learn about time management. This was a challenge. I invited him along to a time management workshop and asked him to fill in a time log for at least a week before the session. I knew perfectly well that he wouldn't bother.

Instead, I asked his secretary to complete the log for him. She did, and provided me with the information. On analysis, I identified that he spent too much time on tasks he had never thought about at all. He spent it talking to his boss! An incredible twenty per cent of his time was taken up by casual talk. Some of this time must have been productive. But how much? The point was that my friend had not realized that so much *time* was eroded each week, by his boss. On average, an incredible one day per week! If he could reduce this by only fifty per cent, look what it would do for his productivity.

The point illustrated here is that we can never be quite sure just where our time goes. Our memory is selective, and we only remember those things which cast us in the best light.

Drucker tells a similar story in his book *The Effective Executive*. He recalls how a business colleague knew precisely how he spent his time. Drucker talked to his colleague's personal assistant about the problem. Drucker's colleague was amazed to find that he did not, as he had stated, spend all his time 'running his company and thinking through strategic issues', but in fact spent it 'charging around the factory floor' progress chasing for business friends who required rush jobs.

It is amazing how much time we can spend doing things of which we are unaware. We select only those things that we wish to recall. We carefully filter out our own personal 'time wasters'.

If we were really critically aware and wished to admit to our 'poor time management behaviour' we might be able to take the necessary action to improve it and reduce time spent on unimportant non-productive work. We might even stop doing work that we pay others to do, and let them get on with it!

Keeping a time log helps us to identify those things that take up our time. It helps, because if we adhere to completing the log at specified times throughout the day, we can at least get an accurate and reliable record of where our time really goes.

Personal analysis

Work through your time log. Identify the major patterns and trends which appear. Calculate how much of your time is spent on routine tasks: report writing, telephones, talking to colleagues, attending meetings, paperwork, travelling, preparing for meeting customers, etc. The idea is that you develop a list of those things which significantly eat into your time. Include also those things on which you don't think you spend enough time.

Now comes the moment of truth. You have to arrange this list of items into two separate lists. Let's call the first list *'Legitimate time consumers'*, those things which you do each day which add to improving your results and your effectiveness.

The other list, to be labelled *'Time wasters'*, should include those things which consume your time, but add little in terms of individual, departmental or organizational success. In other words, these are the time wasters which distract you from the things you should be doing. The purpose of drawing up these two lists is to help you differentiate between those things which lead to payoffs and those things which lead to time wasting. Let's look at some time wasters.

Meetings

Meetings can take up a great deal of a manager's time. Some meetings he attends have little payoff, others provide him with information and enable him to make decisions which will directly impact upon his key results. Other meetings are no more than a waste of time. They consume time, but add little to performance.

work

ork and administration can be a dreadful waste of time. Although it is important to deal with the routine and ensure that the system keeps ticking over, sometimes the *red tape and bureaucracy* take over. How much of your available time each week do you spend on routine steady-state work? Are you spending too much time on trivia, rather than the really important work?

People

People can be the biggest time waster of all! Think about the last time you were working well at your desk and a colleague called by and started talking. You may have been keen to get on and complete the work, but you were drawn into conversation. Perhaps the conversation was about holidays or moving to a new house, but nevertheless you felt you had to say something, and before you knew it you were distracted from the work on hand. How much of your time do you spend talking to people? It is always more than you think!

Travel

How much time do you spend travelling? If you are a commuter travelling ten miles to and from work each day, your journey could take over two hours a day. This is unproductive time which, when subtracted from the time you have left after work and sleep, leaves very little time in which to enjoy your leisure and hobbies! Making use of this time, even if it is only reading reports or making casual notes, will give you payoffs.

Let's forget travelling to and from work. What about travel within work? Recently, I was running a time management workshop for a group of senior distribution managers who worked for a large retail chain store. They spent a tremendous forty per cent of their time travelling! To make matters worse they spent most of their time travelling in cars, so they found it impossible to do anything else at the same time.

Strangely enough, one of their problems was that they often arrived at a depot or a store to find a phone message asking them to shoot back to head office because of a sudden crisis. They seemed to travel a great deal all over the country, but much of their time was wasted, because staff from HQ could not contact them. A car phone would have saved these managers a great deal of time. They had never considered it! Even a pager would have helped them cut down on their biggest time waster.

If travel is an essential part of the job, many managers take with them and use a dictaphone to ensure that they at least note problems they have to solve throughout the day. Many dictate reports and letters. Others use it as an *aide-mémoire*.

Many managers are reluctant to use dictaphones because they feel 'silly' or feel they require training. Making a note of thoughts as they pass through your head can be a real winner. You would be amazed how many good ideas are lost for ever because they are not noted down. Now there is no excuse for this.

Unclear objectives

Many managers confuse being busy with achieving something of value. Witness 'the white tornado'. He is not a mythical figure, but a real person who seems constantly overworked. We all know one. He is very keen to be noticed. But he confuses being busy and rushing about with being effective. The 'white tornado' is a manager who is keen to be noticed! When you talk to him and ask him, 'How is work?' he tells you he is up to his eyes in it! Then he speeds off with handfuls of paper – hence the name – dashing here there and everywhere, wearing out shoe leather, diving in and out of lifts, rushing to and from meetings, etc. Shirt unbuttoned and perspiration running down his forehead, the 'white tornado' truly confuses efficiency and effectiveness.

We don't have to witness the energetic 'tornado', there are cases nearer home, where we can see problems with staff working harder instead of smarter. They put in long hours but achieve very little. They confuse attendance with performance.

One company for whom I worked had an informal competition every night. The middle management group were situated on the fourth floor of an office building and never left before their boss, even if it meant staying until eight o'clock. They thought they were creating the right image! They did. They created the image that the normal eight hours during the day were insufficient in which to do their work. When the senior manager came to make a senior appointment for the department, he chose an outside candidate because he felt the internals could not manage their time. The first task he set for the new recruit was to sort out the management team, and see to it that they attended a time management workshop!

Self-imposed time wasters

Although we might not like to admit it, the biggest problems we have with time management are to do with managing ourselves. Most time management problems are not imposed by others, but by ourselves.

Let us have a look at our time each day. There are three demands on our time: the boss, the system, and ourselves.

Many managers state that they do not control their time. They do. They just do not control their *tasks*. Many tasks are imposed by others. How we use our time to achieve them is up to us. We have some discretion as to how and when to do work.

How much discretion you have will depend upon your position in the hierarchy and the nature of the job. If you are relatively junior and occupy an administrative role, the tasks *imposed by your boss* will take up more time than if you were someone more senior. The reason for this is that you may have relatively little experience and need guidance and structure.

Take an example of two administrators who are both chiefly involved in meetings management. Both occupy the position of meetings secretary. Both have to attend set meetings. Their functions and key tasks are to make notes of the proceedings, which will later become the basis for concise minutes. Both are aware of their responsibilities and their tasks. Both are aware of the time constraints. However, the degree to which these two people structure and *use* their time, will influence the degree to which they achieve their objectives.

One administrator may be in the habit of postponing the task of creating a 'first draft' of the minutes, and choose to do other things, which are not perhaps high priority items. The other administrator, recognizing that the first draft stage is the key, may start on the task first thing in the morning. He may well have finished at lunchtime, whereas his less successful counterpart is still trying to motivate himself to do the job.

Even though the work of both administrators is dictated and *imposed* by others, they do have some freedom in which to complete their work. Time, and how it is used or misused will influence the degree to which they achieve their tasks.

Many managers fail to see that they are responsible for and can influence how they use their time. Some claim that 'the system', whether computerized, manual or paperwork, eats into their time, and stops them getting on with work in their key result areas. The *system imposed tasks* again create tasks and responsibilities, but the 'system' does not dictate how the manager *uses* his time to feed the system with the relevant information.

The area that I feel every manager should concentrate upon is what we can call *self-imposed tasks*. Each day you could look at the time you spend at work and ask yourself, 'How many tasks do I have to complete which are my sole responsibility?' These should exclude tasks imposed by your boss and the system. The answer to the question will vary depending upon your job, your status and the organization in which you work. But the important point is you have *total* control of how you use *your* time to achieve these goals. You decide.

Taking personal responsibility

Blaming others and putting responsibility elsewhere will not help you achieve the task, but it will help others create the right impression about you, that you seek excuses for non-performance.

Managers are expected to be able to work under pressure, to work within tight guidelines. If you are not prepared to examine how you use your time, and seek new techniques and approaches which may mean rejecting some of your old managerial habits, then you will always be time pressured and will never achieve your true potential!

Recognizing that you have three discrete areas in your working life whence tasks emanate, and that you have the responsibility for achieving these tasks in order of priority, should help you to become a better manager.

Time wasters

Before we finish this chapter, it is important for you to look at your two lists again: *Legitimate time consumers* and *time wasters*. You may find that the same subject comes under the two lists. For example, meetings are a forum where managers can create a great deal of change and reach speedy decisions which impact upon the bottom line and influence company performance.

Meetings, on the other hand, can also be the forum for wasting effort, energy and enthusiasm! Clearly, *meetings* themselves are not good or bad, but the way they are structured, and the contribution that members make, will determine their value. Managers who attend meetings and are prepared to make them *positive stimulating forums of debate* are those who will succeed. It is all a matter of attitude.

Consider the following list of key time wasters and ask yourself to what extent they reflect the problems you experience. Think how much of your time you spend on activities such as paperwork, meetings, travelling, planning, delegating and ask yourself whether you should re-orientate yourself to doing something about the situation.

Key time wasters

Paperwork

- Do you spend too much time on the steady-state or routine paperwork?
- Do you keep yourself busy with this rather than spending time on more difficult tasks? If so, what is the cause of the problem?
- Do you find that the paperwork distracts you from other, more important, work?
- Do you find at the end of every month that your pending tray is still full?
- Do you purposely procrastinate, fail to deal with important paper-work, or do you lack the skills, confidence, self-discipline and motivation to do the job?

Meetings

- Do you feel that you have to attend too many meetings and that the value of the decisions reached is disproportionate to the amount of *time* you put into them?
- Are you confusing attendance at meetings with *performance*, i.e. seen to be there, but not adding *value* to the proceedings?
- Do you find that the process of meetings stops the progress you could reach? Do you find that politics takes over from business? Are you not prepared to intervene and influence the outcome?

Telephone calls

- Does the telephone rule and dictate your work and tasks during the day?
- Do you feel that you have little control over the phone?

Inability to say 'no'

- Do you feel pressured to say 'yes' when others ask you to do work?
- Do you have difficulty being assertive and stating your true feelings when asked to take on additional duties?
- Do you take on additional work from others because you have difficulty saying 'no'?

People

- Does the presence of others distract you from your work?
- Do you let others interrupt and stop you when you are working on key projects?
- Do you fall to the whims and tactics of the organization drifter?

Procrastination

- Do you often find it difficult to apply yourself to a task? Do you find this more difficult with high priority work?
- Do you find it difficult to do the routine and mundane?
- Do you tend to apply your talents to those tasks which you find interesting and rewarding?

Unclear goals and priorities

- Do you find it difficult to define your *key result areas*?
- Have you clearly assessed the *key results* and *priorities* you wish to achieve over the next six months?
- Do you find that *urgent trivia* takes over from the *important work*?
- Do you find conflict among the goals and priorities you set?

Delegation

- Do you find that you have a great deal of work to complete, but find it difficult allocating it to your staff?

- Are you clear on the *precise criteria* by which you can delegate?
- Are you the subject of over-delegation, or do you have work delegated up from your subordinates?

Stress

- Do you constantly find it difficult to achieve your results, and feel that the anxiety generated has a negative effect on your performance?
- Do you feel that time pressures create too much personal stress?
- Have you identified your personal stressors and taken the necessary action to reduce their intensity?

Career planning

- Have you developed a plan of 'where you go from here'?
- Have you identified clear career goals?
- What action can you take to realize your career potential and life goals?

The above are just some of the areas with which the following chapters will deal. These factors have been identified as significant time wasters by many managers. The strategies for eradicating these time wasters, are ultimately influenced by the most important ingredient of all, your commitment to get more out of the working day.

A positive attitude and a commitment to change the way you work, to develop self-discipline and plan your goals is the real key. The chapters which follow should help you to highlight those areas where you have to focus your initial efforts in order to improve your performance.

Chapter 4

Analysis: assessing your time management behaviour

There are *four* stages of analysis by which you can examine your time management behaviour.

The first stage

The first stage was introduced in the previous chapter. It is based on the daily planner and this level of analysis is concerned with identifying the key activities which consume our time. We then work on reducing the time spent on time wasters and increase our efforts on positive payoff activities.

We may come to the conclusion that we spend too much time on routine paperwork and in meetings, but insufficient on objective setting and making contingency plans for the future. We can then take action to spend our time doing things which lead to personal and organizational success, and reject the time wasters!

This level of analysis identifies tasks. To go further, we have to assess the degree to which something positive comes out of an activity. We could have sat through a meeting all morning and have done little apart from progressing through routine business. If we are honest, we will assess the 'opportunity cost' of that meeting and not repeat the experience, unless the agenda changes to items of greater or higher priority, or other desirable changes take place.

This 'activity' or 'task' approach to examining how and where we use our time helps us a great deal to cut out the time wasters and develop new managerial habits.

The second stage: added value!

At this stage of analysis, we should introduce the concept of *added value*. Can we identify those tasks, or activities which take up our time, *and* which clearly add value to the product or service we provide? If we find the value of participating in or pursuing a particular activity is minimal or zero, we must ask ourselves, 'Would my time not be better spent elsewhere?'

If the added value of performing a particular activity, i.e. team building and delegation, is *high*, then we are spending our time in the best way. We should ask ourselves whether the value added from performing an activity is positive or negative, and act accordingly.

However, before we reject activities which we think do not add value, we have to ask: is the value gained to be realized in the *long*, or the *short*, term? Often, managers spend a great deal of time on trivial work which adds no value in the longer term, but are not keen to be involved in other activities which they do not perceive to have a higher payoff, or value to the company, in the same term.

They may not be aware of the possible results of their action, which shows lack of foresight, or they may lack the motivation because the investment in time and energy is more than they are prepared to give. Getting the balance right is difficult, but the value added concept is one which should always be considered when analysing time consumers and time wasters! It is a good criterion for rejecting time wasters.

The value added argument is particularly important when one considers the activities of the staff who work for us. What activities can we perform with them, which will help them add value to everything they do?

Do not forget, managers are judged not just by their expertise and individual achievements, but by how they encourage, motivate and achieve through their team. Team building is the key to effective management, and identifying specific actions which can be taken by managers to get their team to add value to everything they do, in either the long or short term, is imperative.

The third stage

How much of your time do you spend on work which could be classed as rework or 'doing work over'? Believe me, more time than you think!

Errors!

How much time do you spend each week correcting errors? These errors could have been created by you, but also could arise elsewhere! How often do you have to go through a report and rewrite? How often do you say to yourself, 'That will do'? As you put the report away, you know you will have to do it again, but you think you might just get away with it this time.

How often do you write a letter, send it to the typing pool, and know that there are still some serious inaccuracies that need to be corrected?

Technology and lazy managers

Managers can become very lazy. Prior to the advent of the electronic office and word processors, managers spent time ensuring that the written communications were 'right first time', before sending them to the typing pool.

Research suggests that the number of drafts has increased since word processors were introduced. In many companies, first or second draft letters were the order of the day. Since the introduction of WPs, the number of average drafts has increased three- or four-fold. The material and content of letters and reports has stayed constant, but the ability to change documents easily has created a great deal of flexibility and, with it, rework.

Managers think that this has given them additional flexibility and an opportunity to improve their output, but it has also created the opportunity for giving rework to others. Knowing how easy it is to change a document has fostered a casual attitude. Secretarial staff are spending more of their time reworking the mistakes of others, than becoming more productive. Although the aim of office automation was to increase productivity, in many cases this has simply not happened. Instead of the output of documents increasing, it has remained the same, but more drafts are being processed for each document. The quality of the documentation has remained constant, and not improved.

Right second time

The 'I will do it right next time' attitude creates many time management problems for others! Trying to assess how often we repeat tasks is important, because it has a bearing on the time we spend doing something positive, such as planning and *preventing errors occurring*!

Inspection

How much of your time do you devote to inspecting the quality of your own work or that of others? If you are involved in a great deal of inspection, you may not be reworking errors, but you are spending a large part of your time looking for them!

This means that some errors exist! But they shouldn't exist, not if we have done work *right first time*. When we talk about inspection, we refer to activities such as, checking a report, reworking figures for a budget, checking the details of a contract, reading through letters before signing them, rereading job descriptions, checking salary slips. The list is endless.

Spotting errors

The reason we inspect work is we feel there might be a significant error in it. If this is so, we may feel that we should do a really good job and 'inspect the hell out of it'. You may even decide to take work home, to inspect quality into it and errors out! You will notice, the more time you spend inspecting errors, the more you will find. If you normally devote three hours per day to inspection, and decide to double it, what will be the end product? You have guessed it, you have spotted more errors! In fact, we could spend all day inspecting this and that, and find even more errors, but will this one activity help us become better managers?

To some extent it does. But managers are judged by the *quality* of their performance. This means the product or service they provide should meet some desired specification. Inspection helps the manager achieve the desired level of quality. But is this the way he should spend his time? No. He should prevent errors instead.

Prevention

Instead of reworking errors and inspecting quality into his work, he should be more positive. He should spend time *preventing* errors occurring. Clearly, the more time taken preventing errors, the less there are that have to be reworked. This, in turn, means less activities that have to be inspected!

Trying to double the time spent on prevention will help cut down on the negative time wasting activities, *reworking* and *inspection*.

A case: The Personnel Department

Some time ago, I worked with a company which had a number of quality problems. As part of the quality programme, I was taking the Personnel Department through a series of management development activities.

We had reached time management. The seven members of the department turned up for the training session, each with their time logs.

I asked them all to go through the major activities in which they had been involved, and asked them to classify the items on which they had spent time under three headings: *error, inspection* and *prevention*.

On analysis, we found that, on average, the members spent fifty-four per cent of their time *reworking errors* and doing work again, forty-one per cent on *inspection* activities and five per cent on *preventative* action.

No wonder they did not achieve anything! No wonder they came into work at 8 a.m. and stayed late. Little wonder morale was low!

The most surprising thing about the department was that its members knew they spent too much time in meetings, and on routine paperwork, but they had never before focused on their work and analysed it using these three criteria. We dug deeper to find out the cause of the problem!

Line managers

Whatever personnel managers say, it is extremely difficult for them to become more than a reactive service department. These departments exist to meet the needs of others in the organization. In the above case, the department was working continuously with line managers, or, rather, in spite of them!

Personnel provided the usual recruitment and selection services as well as induction and appraisal facility. The personnel manager was bright and had sought to introduce many new initiatives into the company. She had often tried to train line managers to understand the problems with recruitment and selection, and get them to appreciate the huge costs associated with either appointing the wrong person, or attracting and shortlisting the wrong group from which to select.

Right second time

On many occasions, posts had been re-advertised and interviews held time and time again. It transpired that line managers were not spending any time at all preparing documentation for personnel. They were using job descriptions that were years old and didn't reflect the changing nature of some of the engineering posts. They were not taking care and being selective in using the material. The consequence of this behaviour was rework for others!

Some line managers were guilty of not training their supervisors in the use of the disciplinary code. Consequently, some staff were unfairly dismissed, and this created costly administrative rework and other costs for the company.

Generally, because the relationship between the line and staff function (personnel) was poor, the Personnel Department was suffering. The only way to remedy the situation, and reduce the chances of spending all its time in the future reworking line management's errors, was to *invest time* in developing the appropriate relationship with the other managers. This we could define as *preventative* action.

We originally set a target to double the time the personnel people spent on prevention type activities, and we knew that in the end this would reduce errors and inspection. Getting closer to the managers, and spending time explaining the problems the department faced, the quality of the service it could provide if given detailed and *accurate* information, looking at company priorities and forgetting departmental differences and negative stereotypes, were all factors which helped reduce the amount of time they spent on correcting, rather than preventing, errors.

We asked all those involved in the exercise to think before they started a task:

'What is the best use of my time right now, and how can I ensure I spend time *preventing* errors arising in the future?'

This type of analysis helps many managers focus upon their key result areas in a different way. Thinking about your work in this way should help you spend less time firefighting, and more time planning and preventing problems occurring.

The fourth stage

The final level of analysis should help managers gain some sort of perspective in what they do. They should assess how much of their time they spend doing or being engaged in, the following types of activity.

Administrative activities

This could be defined as the routine, the steady-state administrative tasks that have to be maintained. Although this work is important, it may distract you from the high priority work!

Communications activities

This includes those activities that require giving instructions, going to meetings, talking on the telephone, consulting with others, etc. It is important that all managers spend some of their time communicating, but it must be orientated towards achieving results. If we are not careful, communication can become an aim in itself, rather than a means to an end.

Operations activities

This encapsulates all those things that are connected with non-managerial duties but are directly related to the 'operation'. In industry, it might mean dealing with a technical problem or helping in your original area of expertise.

After promotion, many managers are accused of not spending enough time on 'managerial type' activities. Instead, they revert to their specialism. They stay psychologically, and physically in some circumstances, in their area of initial training. They may occupy their time doing things 'they are no longer paid to do'. This gives these managers a means of security. They are in an environment that they understand, and that they can control. They will not be required to do things that either they do not understand, or cannot control. They are safe because they absorb themselves in their first love!

Management: achieving results through people

Management is the art and science of managing results through people. Many managers accept this, but still spend too much time in operational activities. At this level of analysis, it is clear that they are wasting time if they spend a disproportionate amount of their time doing things that others are paid to do!

Managerial activities

How much of your time do you spend managing people? Activities include giving instructions, training where necessary, coaching and mentoring, motivating and listening to problems, etc. It is clear that managers are paid to manage, but the time they should spend on this is usually sacrificed by spending too much time on administration and operational work.

Executive activities

Executive activities are referred to as time devoted to thinking, planning, and organizing for the future. This means spending time decision making, thinking, solving problems, planning, researching.

We never spend enough time doing this sort of work, the reason being that we have too much work that falls into the *rework* or *inspection* categories. We never seem to have the time to think about the opportunities offered by *tomorrow*, because we are so busy worrying about *yesterday's* problem.

You will note that your major work activities will not slot neatly into the above categories. In some cases, there will be overlaps, especially between communicating and managing activities, but we must bear in mind the following:

- There are a number of different levels by which we can understand our management of time. The most basic is identifying activities which take up our time. *Identifying the time wasters* and assessing the percentage of our day we spend doing certain tasks helps us reformulate our thoughts, and take action to spend less time on activities that add little to our key result areas.
- The second stage of analysis tells us that we should look at all these activities, and assess the degree to which we *add value and achieve our key results*, by participating in them. If we gain little value from an experience or work activity, we should cease it, and increase our efforts and devote our energy to those things which add value and facilitate the achievement of our major goals and objectives.
- The third level of analysis helps us *examine our work in terms of error, inspection or prevention*. The purpose of this approach is to spend proportionately more time on prevention than on firefighting activities.
- The fourth level of analysis examines how much time we spend on activities which broadly fall under the headings of *administrative, communications, operations, managerial and executive*. The purpose of examining how much time we devote to these activities is to get the balance right, especially by reducing routine administrative work, by delegating to others and spending more time on managerial and executive tasks.

No one level of analysis is better than the others, but it is worth while to look at different approaches and integrate these approaches into our action plan for change, which is the subject of the next chapter!

Chapter 5

Taking action

Now that you have gone through the analysis of 'how your time is used', let's see what positive action you can take to get twelve hours out of the eight-hour day!

Later, we will look at strategies, techniques and tips for helping you to deal with specific problems, such as managing meetings and curing the paperwork problem. But just now we are painting the broad picture and identifying some of the important principles which you should use to plan and use your time more constructively.

Attitude

Words and workshops do not by themselves necessarily change the behaviour of managers. However many sessions, workshops or seminars a manager attends, however many books he reads on time management, the extent to which he will learn and practise these new behaviours is related directly to his commitment to trying out new ideas!

If he has a negative attitude and does not believe that a system will work, it will not. If he is positive and believes that the system will work, it will. The secret of any manager's becoming an expert practitioner and advocate of time management lies in his *commitment* to the system. If he is committed to making the time management system work, he will succeed!

He also needs an action plan for change. We will talk about this a little later when we discuss the daily planner.

The enthusiastic manager does not wish only to change his own time management habits and behaviour. He realizes that he has a role to play in changing the behaviour and attitudes of others. If he can increase his productivity by thirty to forty per cent, then these actions should have some impact upon his team. He should be able to improve their performance, by following some simple principles!

What will his team expect?

His team may find that he will now spend time talking to them, helping to communicate and agree key result areas. He will give information and feedback on what he considers are 'time wasting' activities, and he will do as much as he can to help the team members achieve their results.

Leading by example

The effective manager knows that others only take the lead when they see a demonstration of how things 'should be'. They need direction and they require a leader to show them the way. Leading by example is the only way by which managers can hope to influence the behaviour and actions of their staff.

Defining the parameters

What principles can we follow which will help us model our behaviour so that we can achieve more each day?

Information

Everyone uses information. Even those who occupy lowly positions within the organization have to use information in order to do their work. This may include interpretation or disseminating information in a form that has *meaning*. All managers deal with information. The *quality* of the decisions they reach is determined by the *reliability* and *accuracy* of the information which they collect, develop and use.

The more senior a manager becomes, the more his ability for generating, collecting, understanding and communicating information must increase. Without an accurate database, it is impossible to guide policy or strive to achieve key goals in a consistent manner.

People

Having information and making decisions is important, but if the manager has only his own resource, himself, to manage, then he is not a manager!

A manager is responsible for getting others to achieve his results. He is judged by his ability to develop and motivate a team of people to do just this. Hence the people dimension. If the manager cannot get others to achieve his targets, he is not very good at his job. Consequently, he has to create special relationships with people, understand their motivational drive, align their key strengths, and diminish their weaknesses, in order to meet his goals in a speedy manner.

This leads us to the final component.

Negotiation

If a manager wants to have someone do something, he must let them know! His communication skills and his ability to influence and persuade others to pursue a course of action are the prerequisites for success. Those who do not possess these skills achieve very little. They are forced to develop other strategies. Those who cannot convince and persuade have to use more structured approaches, and rely more on their position in the hierarchy, i.e. the 'I am the boss' approach.

Managers with good social skills, who display a profound interpersonal competence, are those who can get others to identify with, and meet, specified targets. Negotiation, as a general managerial skill, should never be dismissed as being of secondary importance. It is *vital*. Managers spend much time communicating, and their effectiveness is measured by the degree to which their communication is successful in making things happen!

The four key result areas (KRAs) above help to define the parameters within which a manager can measure himself. He should use the key result programmer (Fig. 5.1) to help him identify where he should be focusing his attention. He should ask himself the following questions:

- What are the key tasks that I should achieve in each of the areas?
- What are the activities and tasks within each area which take up time?
- Is the time spent on the KRA commensurate with the rewards or achievements and value gained?

Completing the key result programmer should help clarify those things which measure and reflect a manager's performance. The advantage of filling in the key results programmer is that it forces him to keep away from woolly and ambiguous work tasks and be more specific. The sections identify key tasks and activities, and then help him appraise the degree to which he is getting value for money for the

Key result areas	Decision making	Information	People	Negotiation
Identify key tasks				
What are key activities?				
Time spent and value gained				

Fig. 5.1 Key result programmer

investment in time and effort he puts into the work. Although decidedly simple, this matrix should take about thirty minutes to complete. Devoting time to this will create many payoffs for those who have not previously identified their KRAs.

Short- and long-term priorities

Now that you have identified your KRAs, it is time to examine your long- and short-term goals. This you achieve by examining the key activities and tasks you aim to complete. Some of these tasks may appear very important, but the payoff generated is minimal to your long-term goals. These are, clearly, activities which you should minimize in the future.

It is relatively easy to forget about your long-term goals because they are so far off that you may think you have plenty of time to achieve them! You are wrong. Sooner or later, that long-term priority is going to need some fairly rapid action. If you leave it too late, and try to cram too much into too little time, you are sure to create many and varied anxieties and stresses for yourself!

Knowing that a goal has to be completed some time in the future is no excuse for not taking decisive action *now*. If you do fail to plan, and think through the steps you will need to take, to meet your long-term goal, you may arrive at a situation where the time you have allocated to the goal is insufficient to meet the target fully.

We are all judged, not only by the degree to which we meet short-term goals, but also how we plan resources to meet our long-term goals. Failing to achieve them suggests we do not possess the strategic overview, and demonstrates that, although we are aware of the importance of meeting long-term goals, we *fail* to manage our time to do so.

As each day passes, these long-term goals come nearer. We reach a stage where, if we have not taken any effective action, we start to panic. We have probably spent far too much time on the short-term goals. The reason for this is that we find them easier to achieve. They are tangible. Let us not spend too much time on short-term objectives, certainly not at the cost of long-term ones. If we do, we shall be confusing short-term efficiency with effectiveness. We have to ensure that we have the balance right. Every day we should take some action, no matter how small, to enable us to work towards our long-term goals. We should adopt the 'step-by-step approach', which will help us achieve the major objectives.

Priorities

Now that you have assessed your priorities, it is time to rank them in order of importance. We should have priorities which relate to:

- decision making;
- information management;
- people, including motivation, training and coaching; and
- negotiation, our ability to influence others.

We should rank our priorities A, B or C. Those priorities we classify as As are those that are of strategic importance. Bs are of operational value and help us achieve our intermediate targets, while Cs relate to the day-to-day routine. Now that these have been ranked, set yourself specific targets over time, and work towards them.

On a day-by-day basis, you can set and *meet* priorities. Certainly, you are never going to achieve the really important items in a few hours, but you can make some progress by breaking down the steps and activities in which you have to engage yourself in order to make the problem or work manageable.

The reason many people never reach their A priority goals is that these goals are too difficult. They set goals that are so difficult that it is impossible to get anywhere near them. The key to achievement lies in breaking the approaches down into *manageable steps*! We will never meet a goal which is too difficult by tackling it head on.

If you have an important report to complete, the sheer size of it may force you to procrastinate. You may say, 'Where do I start?' or 'How am I going to do all this in the time available?' Quite simply, the answer lies in planning ahead and breaking the large project down into realistic and manageable steps. Once you have achieved this, you will find it much easier to meet deadlines. No longer are they unrealistic. You will be able to measure your progress by the activities in which you engage yourself daily. Decide on your priorities on a daily basis, and record them on the daily planner.

Writing a list of priorities is not enough. You should also list them in order of importance, otherwise you will never get down to tackling the problem of achieving them.

Which should I do first?

Some people suggest that they tackle the easy problems first, so they have the rest of the day to allocate to the important issues. This can be a mistake, because it is a strategy adopted by many managers who unwittingly practise *procrastination*.

Several managers have told me about their procrastinating behaviour. They arrive at the office ready for work, and divert themselves from the *important* by dealing with some of the easy problems that land on their desk. They fail to recognize that many of the little problems can be quite time consuming. Everything takes longer than they think!

When they have eventually finished, they have a quick break, a coffee, and start to think about the big problem. The phone may ring and, again, they are diverted from their course of action. Lunch time comes round and they convince themselves that they will start working on the problem at 2 p.m.

Unfortunately, something always happens that requires attention and they put off the work till later that day. When the time comes that they have earmarked for dealing with the problem, they are past their best. They are tired, and frustrated by not achieving what they wanted.

They decide to take the work home. But owing to family commitments, the briefcase is brought back to the office the following morning, unopened from leaving work the previous day. No progress has been made!

Stress, anxiety and time pressures are building up. If managers do not break their bad habits they will feel obliged and pressurized into working excessively on projects over the weekend. Because they do this, their relaxation and leisure time will have been seriously curtailed. They are not properly prepared for the week ahead. Sooner or later, this behaviour will result in others finding out about their inefficiency and ineffectiveness!

The urgent takes over from the important

They have put off doing the most important work. Every manager knows that frequently, the *urgent takes over from the important*. You have to plan *in spite* of this. This requires a discipline that is hard for some to attain. Allocate yourself ten minutes at the beginning of the day to tackle the problem. You will find that ten minutes is sufficient to get started and, soon, you will be flying through the work.

Even better, get to work an hour early. No, not every day, but certainly on those days which you have put aside for high priority work. The distractions will be nil, or at least be only *self-imposed*. Others will not be there to distract you, and you will be surprised how much you can achieve when the telephone is not ringing and people do not pop in for a quick chat! You would be amazed how much time is wasted each day by the early morning rituals of chatting, reading the paper, answering the phone and getting warmed up for the day ahead.

When your colleagues arrive, you can pat yourself on the back for achieving so much. If you were to look at the productivity curve of a manager, you would find that most of the work is achieved in the morning. Things cool down just before, and after, lunch and generally grind to a standstill as the end of the day approaches.

Confusing performance with attendance!

Staying late at the end of the day does not really help, because you are tired and will probably need regular 'caffeine injections', cups of coffee to keep you alert. An architect friend of mine has a novel theory of diminishing returns. He feels that if he stays from 5 p.m. to 6 p.m. he is probably productive for only twenty to twenty-five minutes. From 6 p.m. to 7 p.m. this falls to ten minutes, and every hour after that productive time falls by fifty per cent. This illustrates the classic mistake of confusing attendance at work with performance – the two are not necessarily the same.

The day after

Staying late does not affect just our performance that day, but also the day after. We arrive at the office tired and jaded, and, more importantly, not in the frame of mind to do the job right. How often do managers complain about staying late at the office for two or three hours? I prefer managers to talk about what they have achieved, not the time spent sitting in a chair worrying about how they are going to complete the work.

The daily planner

The only way to break out of this negative spiral is to use the daily planner. Make a commitment now to use the daily planner and complete it each day, before you start work. Some managers fill in the planner the night before. It is their last task before they go home. They

---

THE DAILY PLANNER

Priority Ranking:		Priority Register:	
1.	6.	1.	6.
2.	7.	2.	7.
3.	8.	3.	8.
4.	9.	4.	9.
5.	10.	5.	10.

Must Do	Should Do	Like To Do	Telephone
1.	1.	1.	1.
2.	2.	2.	2.
3.	3.	3.	3.
4.	4.	4.	4.
			5.
			6.
			7.
			8.

Meetings:	Time	Objectives	Action	Decision

Fig. 5.2 The daily planner

make a reasonable appraisal of the work they have to do, decide on their priorities, and list them in rank order (see Fig. 5.2).

Must, should and like

The 'must, should and like' principle helps managers add an element of reality to their work. Divide work up into work you *must* do, work you *should* do and the work you *like* to do. You will find that the work or task which falls under 'must' is high priority, and because of its nature, difficult. You may find that it is non-routine. You may not have tackled it before and there is no one best way of doing it. It has to be dealt with early on.

Work which falls under the 'should' criterion is that work which is not A priority work, but should have some impact upon your immediate results. Work you 'like' doing is work you probably feel competent and able to do. You probably enjoy this work and like doing it. This is where the danger lies. Managers can spend a disproportionate time on work they *like* doing, rather than work which they *must* do. Beware of this pitfall and fill in the daily planner now. Be aware of your likes and dislikes and do not let them guide your choice.

Alan Lakein, in his book *How to Get Control of Your Time and Your Life*, suggests that you should allocate 75% of your time to the work you *must* do, 20% to the work you *should* do, and 5% to the work you *like* doing. Getting the balance right is also important. There is little likelihood that you will be able to pursue A priority work all the time.

The 80/20 rule

You will probably find that there are two types of manager in your organization. One type are those who fly about all the time being very busy, devoting 80% of their time to achieving 20% of their results. The effective manager, on the other hand, is the one who assesses his priorities and devotes 20% of his time to achieving 80% of the key results. Getting the balance right is easy, though many fail to do so.

Satisfaction and reward

Someone, somewhere, once said that all managerial work was interesting and rewarding. This is not necessarily true. A great deal of a manager's work is boring, uninteresting, mundane, etc. but it is still of high priority to the company. Do not confuse priorities with interest.

Work which may give little satisfaction, perhaps due to its routine nature, may add considerably to the results of a company. The biggest single problem which many managers face is not knowing when to draw the line with work which does not interest them.

The daily planner: a case study

A particular company was concerned that its managers were not managing their time well. The company decided to take action, run a series of management development sessions, and asked the managers to complete and adhere to the discipline of the daily planner.

They also reduced the daily planner to pocket size. Then they created a 'house rule'. Each manager had to keep the planner up to date, and, if asked by other managers, had to produce it there and then. At first this met with some resistance, but the company decided to continue the exercise.

The result was that managers started to think clearly about their priorities and their daily tasks. The exchange of information spread. Managers talked over lunch about their daily plans. In some departments, they recognized that two or three people were in effect doing the same job. There was a great deal of repetition which represented a tremendous waste of resources. The exercise reduced waste and rework to a minimum.

Meetings and telephone calls

There is sufficient space in the daily planner to make notes on meetings to be attended and phone calls which have to be made. Focusing the managers' attention on meetings, and asking them to make brief notes of their objectives, the likely decisions and action to be taken, helped them to clarify their reasons for attendance, and to improve the process of decision making.

Too much time can be spent on the phone. On analysis, many find that a great deal of their telephone conversation is 'social' in nature. They lose the focus, or become tangential in their discussions and spend far too long on the phone. They confuse being sociable with performance. Of course, we cannot always launch into business straight away, and people do like to ease themselves slowly into a business conversation, but one must be aware when chat is taking over and is detrimental to work.

Completing the appropriate section in the daily planner should help you to focus your attention on your objectives during phone conversations, and enable you to use your time in a more productive manner.

Priority register

The priority register is the last column on the daily planner. When it is completed it signifies the extent to which the previous day's priorities have been met. These should be recorded and assessed before completing the priority ranking.

If you have been successful in implementing your plan, you should have been able to achieve all your A priority work. What will be left are Bs and Cs. These should be integrated into your current work plan.

Balance and flexibility

A final point on the daily planner. One should always plan for contingencies. One should try to be flexible. The idea behind the plan is *not* to cram as much as you can into the day, but, rather, to deal with the *priority* work in a manner which will pay premiums in time savings.

You will not always be able to do high priority work. There will be occasions when it is best to deal with B and C priorities, but what you must be aware of is that this must not become a way of life. The daily planner should help you get more out of the day. It is a flexible tool, so use it as such.

WITBUOMTRN?

Finally, a golden rule Lakein suggests which should be followed by every manager is to ask himself at intervals during each day:

WHAT IS THE BEST USE OF MY TIME RIGHT NOW?

If his time could be spent more effectively doing other things, what stops him doing them? The second part of this book addresses these issues, confronts the major problems which the manager faces, and suggests strategies he can use to get twelve hours out of the eight-hour day!

Part 2

Strategies for achieving results

Chapter 6

Procrastination . . . taking action!

Why is it, when we are so busy and up to our eyes in important work, we can spend time making and drinking coffee or talking on the phone, anything rather than working? Why is it that we can always find 1001 things to do which keep us away from the really important work? How can we immerse ourselves in trivia when a major project is waiting to be completed?

We get sucked into procrastinating or simply putting off the important, high priority work and keeping ourselves busy with the humdrum.

If you feel you suffer from this big time waster you are not alone. We all procrastinate at one time or other. Think back to your student days or ask any student how easy he finds it to complete essays or projects on time. Most admit that they spend too much time making coffee and thinking negatively about the difficulty of the project – and the consequences of non-completion – rather than getting down to the real work.

Thinking and procrastination

Many managers suffer from the same problem. Either they don't spend enough time thinking through their priorities and plans, or they waste time using thinking as an excuse for inaction!

Many use 'thinking' as an excuse for not getting down to the really important work which they find dull or difficult. This chapter of the book is a case in point. How easy it would have been to find a reason to leave the study and talk with my wife, phone a friend or make yet another coffee! At the end of the day, the chapter would not have been completed and the deadlines set would not be achieved. The anxiety of non-completion may have generated pressures culminating in *personal stress*.

Stress

We *manufacture* our own stress levels. Stress is not imposed from outside. We create the environment within which we handle the 'pressures'. One of these pressures is setting targets but not reaching them, in other words procrastination.

We create many of the pressures ourselves. One such, which we *can* control, but sometimes allow to get the better of us, is the procrastination problem. We often fail to recognize that we are the masters of our destiny, and that we can do something about procrastination. Stop and think for a moment and be prepared to confront your procrastination habits! What stops you performing work on time? What is it about your personal and managerial habits that prevents you achieving results?

What besides procrastination?

Is procrastination the only reason for failing to complete work on time? No. There are many reasons for non-completion of work. Perhaps we have set targets which were not realistic. We may have set goals which were non-achievable without special assistance. We may have lacked clarity and given insufficient thought to the fine detail or the enormity of the problem, or possibly we lacked the motivation, discipline and commitment to make things happen!

Problems which arise from difficulties with goal clarity can soon be put right, but problems which relate to, and emanate from, self-direction and motivation, are very difficult to solve, for the simple reason that *you* are stopping yourself achieving the goals.

Commitment

It's hard to take, isn't it, accepting responsibility for your own actions? Many managers find it very difficult to admit that they are their own worst enemy.

If managers following any action plan or using daily planning diaries fail to manage their time more effectively, it is usually because they lack sufficient *commitment*.

If commitment is missing, managers will never change the way they work. We are not talking about managers changing the way they think, rather identifying action as the most important factor. We need to help them change their *attitudes, skills* and, most important of all, *behaviour*. Your results are determined not only by what you achieve, but also what you help others to achieve. You have to influence the behaviour of others, and the best way to do this is by example. If *you* stop procrastinating, others will learn and imitate your behaviour.

Why is it that managers who lack commitment and self-motivation fail to kill the procrastination problem? They do not confront their own behaviour or question the way they do things. They fail to ask themselves why some of their colleagues achieve results, and others do not. What differentiates the 'procrastinator' from his successful counterpart?

Perception

The effective manager is one who has a clear idea of his goals and how he hopes and intends to fulfil his key result areas. More than this, he is aware of his skills and behaviours. In other words, he has a clear and accurate idea of his abilities as a manager. I am not talking about expertise or about technical skills or professional knowledge, but those skills which separate the 'achiever' from the 'poor performer'. One of the key areas is self-perception, to know one's own *strengths* and *weaknesses*, and have a personal plan of action that is concerned with putting right what is wrong.

A manager may not be able to change his behaviour overnight, but if he possesses the skill of self-perception, and has an insight into his own learning process, he will be constantly aware of improving on past performance.

Understanding procrastination

Procrastination creates situations where work that should be completed is put off in favour of other work or activities which have no bearing on key results. Consider the case where a manager has an important report to write, but fails to complete it on time. He may spend his time instead doing work which has a low priority for the organization, perhaps dealing with routine correspondence.

The manager is aware that the 'report' is crucial but still finds it difficult to focus his attention, energy and behaviour to doing this high priority work. Why?

The decision he has made has little to do with rational thought. He knows himself what he should be doing, but prefers to do other work. Why? If he doesn't confront this problem he will find that the consequences could radically affect his whole future.

Often, when managers are engaged on work that is crucial to a department or the organization, they display 'procrastination'. They fail to recognize that this behaviour can destroy all the good work they have put in over the years. They try to cover their tracks by adopting a number of *coping behaviours*.

Coping behaviours

Managers pretend that they are extremely busy. The activities that keep them busy are usually steady-state, routine work. In other words, the work which stops them performing is work which they can cope with easily. This work is typified by being *tangible* and *visible*. The rationale they develop is that their productivity can be equated with the quantity of work they do each day. They forget *quality*. They become obsessed with volume rather than quality. They feel that creating vast quantities of work or output will excuse them from high priority work.

This strategy may work in the short term. Many managers defend their behaviour by spending all their time in 'corrective' activities, correcting and reworking. They avoid the difficult, and spend their time solving minor problems which others could do. They come to enjoy firefighting trivial problems.

Comments they repeat include:

'If only I had enough time, I could get down to the really important work.'

'If the routine work isn't dealt with efficiently, how can we ever hope to achieve the really important stuff.'

To paraphrase Peter Drucker in *The Effective Executive*: '. . . they have confused efficiency with effectiveness'. They have made themselves super-efficient at the cost of effectiveness. They have failed to realize that:

'. . . ALTHOUGH THEY ARE DOING THE JOB RIGHT, THEY ARE DOING THE WRONG JOB.'

They don't realize that they may have outgrown their potential. They have, to quote the Peter Principle, reached their level of incompetence.

Is incompetence a natural state to which we all rise? Of course not! The symptom of incompetence is only a temporary coping behaviour, although it becomes a way of life for many managers. They constantly seek targets they can achieve and show their worth by completing and generating high output, low priority, work.

Many senior managers recognize this behaviour, usually accept it, and quote the Peter Principle. Because so many managers exhibit this defect, senior managers have been educated into *accepting* this as the norm! They say, 'Bill is a little slow at picking up and dealing with some of the strategic issues, but he is a great worker. He has some difficulty dealing with the higher priority work, but he does produce good results on the routine lines, and he is always busy and very efficient in his line of work'.

Many managers come to expect this behaviour of their staff. When it manifests itself, it is rewarded by not being challenged. Many managements fail to identify the *real* cause of the problem, and suffer the consequences. It is hardly surprising to find whole management teams struck with the *efficiency* bug.

Failure to perform, and complete, high priority work, is forgiven in some organizations, especially where a manager is elderly. However, a younger manager could destroy his promotion prospects, and even lose his job.

Fear of failing

There is no one major cause of procrastination, but the fear of failure may account for the way many managers behave. They fear failure because they will be judged by their performance. They do not want others to judge their performance negatively. Ultimately, this results in the manager being prepared to enter only into situations or problems that he will find easy to deal with. So he always wins. No one questions his proven ability. He always achieves what he sets out to achieve.

Consequently, the fear of failure leads to a situation where the manager is not prepared to take risks for the simple reason that *risk* itself is a variable which can create failure. Managers then tend to pursue activities that are categorized as low risk. These activities tend to be low priority and related to efficiency, rather than effectiveness, criteria. Putting off risky ventures, and pursuing the mundane, safeguards the reputation of the manager, but at a cost. The cost relates to, and is equated with, learning and self-development, which ultimately hinders promotion prospects.

Managers who are unwilling to try new ways of working, who are risk avoiders, to save face, reputation and credibility, are never able to examine their true potential. They use procrastination as a vehicle for postponing the admission of not being successful.

Managers whose behaviour falls under the umbrella of 'procrastination' are constantly under the illusion that they are successful. But, they are only successful in solving problems that are routine, low risk, and efficiency based. They never pursue the high risk, strategic issues because they fear failing, and being under the scrutiny of their colleagues and peers.

Self-image

Often, managers who portray this behaviour are afraid of facing up to their inadequacies. They are afraid to try anything new in case it results in embarrassing failure. Their self-image would be tarnished. If this behaviour is repeated over time, self-worth suffers.

The fallacy of this approach is the belief that one's work performance, albeit in one discrete area, is a reflection of one's self-worth as a person. This is clearly nonsense. Here, the manager lacks a perspective of his contribution to the organization, and the worth of all the managerial activities that he performs.

This also says something about the work ethic in the West, which equates 'work' with 'success' in life. Work may be a central life interest, but clearly, managers must find time to develop other aspects of their personality, and other abilities, in order to achieve an effective and balanced lifestyle.

They must seek to get some balance back into their life, and this means thinking clearly about their 'overall' contribution and recognizing that self-worth is not simply a mirror reflection of work activities!

The coping mechanisms which many employ are to protect their perceived self-worth by avoiding those things that can create a negative self-image. This means avoiding work that is non-routine, high priority, risk orientated. The pursuit of the mediocre and the thirst for volume at the cost of quality holds back many from achieving their full potential.

The angelic manager

Many are concerned that to achieve a goal means they have to display the qualities of an angel. They read of managers who display a zero defect mentality, and feel they have to emulate this performance at all times. They become perfectionists.

Instead of using the 'balanced' approach to work, they decide that every action they take must be 100% right first time.

There is nothing wrong with adopting this approach to many managerial problems, but the principle of right first time must be related to the end result. Spending a disproportionate amount of time on trivial work, or that with minimum payoffs for the organization in the long term, means that there is less time for the really important work.

Managers should spend their time obeying the Pareto Principle, expending 20% of their effort on 80% of their key results. Many adopt the opposite approach, spending 80 or 90% of their time achieving 20% of their results. Which do you think is the more effective?

Again, a perspective of balance must be brought into play. Managers identifying their key result areas should spend time trying to achieve their optimum position. There is a trade off between efficiency and effectiveness. Recognizing this, and ensuring that a balance is achieved, is what differentiates the effective manager from the ineffective.

Satisfaction

The thrill in achieving goals has a great deal to do with a feeling of accomplishment. Managers often equate performance with *satisfaction*. This is frequently not the case. Work which might not lead to a high degree of job satisfaction can nevertheless be work which has a high priority for the company.

Getting the balance right is sometimes a matter of experience and judgement. Managers with a low threshold for boredom can reduce their capacity to achieve results by concentrating only upon what they perceive as important, the measure for which is the interest the work generates for them.

It is comparatively easy to spend time with staff, and train them to take over your routine duties, instead of doing the work yourself. Doing it yourself may save you time in the short term, but how often do you spend time on the same repetitive work, when you could have invested your time, delegated work to others, trained them in best practice, and reduced your time on low priority tasks? Many wrongly feel that the work which gives *psychological* rewards is work which the organization values. Too often we forget the balance between work that is important to the company, and work that stimulates, excites and interests us.

Anger

Another major cause of procrastination is aggression or anger. We may find that some managers purposely procrastinate. They may have some deep-seated hostility to others, which is reflected by postponing the matter at hand, or 'procrastinating'.

For instance, a middle manager may react unfavourably to the demands of his senior manager. Through resentment, or other problems related to interpersonal conflict, he may decide to delay, halt or postpone work that his superior requires. The precise reasoning is unimportant, but we must all recognize that this problem exists. Difficulties related to politics and personalities create more problems in organizations than we would care to accept.

Skills

Procrastination can be created by managers experiencing dissonance between the skills they ought to have and those they do have. The desire for achieving results, coupled with motivation, may be present, but if the manager lacks the requisite attitudes, skills and knowledge to do the job well, his confidence and actions may be temporarily disturbed. Managers who are aware of their skill deficiencies, and who take positive action to redress their skill imbalances, are those who suffer little from procrastination.

Managers with commitment, but lacking in confidence and skills, may be sucked into the 'fear of failure' mode and find it difficult to break out of it. The only way to combat this problem, once and for all, is to develop a positive and proactive approach to skill acquisition through a formalized, relevant and suitable programme of training.

The first step

As with all time management problems, the first step which must be taken is to acknowledge the fact that you, the manager, are responsible for influencing your own destiny. Although some of the tasks in which you are engaged are agreed and imposed by others (namely your boss, the system and other, senior, managers), you will find that there is some time in the day which is directly under your control. The first step is recognizing that you can take action to redress the time imbalance. You may not influence the tasks, but the time at your disposal is within your control.

Acknowledging the cause of your procrastination begins the process that enables you to take control of your time and your life. If you feel that, some of the reasons for procrastination include:

- fear of failing,
- trying to maintain an unrealistic self-image,
- striving to be the angelic manager,
- negative use of anger,
- skills deficiency,

It is time to develop new, more innovative, methods of controlling your time. Coming to terms with your reasons for procrastination and being prepared to take action to solve the problem are the pre-requisites for success.

Fear

Managers should confront their fears head on. Encouraging them to take risks within defined constraints is an important management development technique. How else can managers progress and develop?

Self-image

Try to avoid the belief that every action you take will influence the image of you which others form. Their perception of your errors, mistakes and problems and your perception of the same problems may bear little resemblance in real life. Develop a sense of balance – don't take your work too seriously.

Perfection

Avoid trying to be the perfect manager. You will disappoint yourself and others. Successful managers learn as much from the mistakes they make, as the problems they solve.

Frustration

Forget 'getting even'. Forget the politics of yesterday. Spend today constructing a better tomorrow and use your anger positively.

Skills

When you stop learning you stop living. Skill acquisition and identifying the skills you need to function tomorrow are the most important aspects of your job. Learning yesterday's skill is redundant. Identify tomorrow's opportunities and train yourself and others to achieve your goals.

Tips for the procrastinator

There are no foolproof methods for solving the procrastination question once and for all, but the following tips should address many of the problems that managers face.

Objectives

Set realistic and achievable goals. They will help you to clarify the position and help you think in realistic terms. The objective you set must be measurable, so that you know when you have attained it. Ask yourself:

'Can I achieve the objective, bearing in mind resource constraints and time scales?'

Managers often find it difficult to apply themselves to the task on hand. The reason is that they look at the size of the venture or the problems, and fail to scale them down into small achievable steps.

Examining the number and sequence of activities that you need to pursue before solving a problem is a valuable planning aid. Thinking through the key issues and setting small measurable steps is the secret to achieving the long-term goal. Some people spend a great deal of effort trying to achieve the task all at once. It is impossible and undesirable to tackle it this way. The risk of failure and demoralization is too great.

Rewards

We have stressed the importance of self-motivation, commitment and discipline. We should reward ourselves when a task is successfully completed. The reward does not have to be large, but sufficient to reflect the success. Lunch at a favourite restaurant, buying a new book, etc., are rewards which can be associated with doing a good job.

It is also possible to set up a system of penalties. The basis of this idea is behaviour modification. Establishing a link between your performance and rewards/penalties acts as a useful form of reinforcement. You start to learn to positively reinforce your positive behaviour and penalize the negative and undesirable.

Start small, aim large

Never tackle an enormous problem in one go. Prepare yourself to work on small components. Set yourself a deadline and achieve what you can. Later on, the components can be fitted into a sequence and give you a broader picture. The difference between this approach and the small steps approach outlined above is that you do not need to tackle the problem in sequence, but do so in sections as the mood takes you.

'Fifteen minutes before lunch'

Make the fifteen minutes before lunch work for you. Ensure that you devote those fifteen minutes to specific action. This may mean writing a report. You may start and have completed half a page before lunch-time – this is usually time when you would be winding down, talking to others.

Fifteen minutes is sufficient to really get on with, and perhaps solve, a problem. When you eventually go to lunch, you will feel better for having tackled the problem and taken action.

You might like to use your fifteen minutes post lunch session to crack on and complete the bulk of your work. This is a technqiue which works only if you really do go for lunch! After fifteen minutes, you need thirty minutes of lunch to think through how you are going to tackle the afternoon session. Working right the way through your lunch break may 'crack' some of the problem, but will not prepare you for a full and productive afternoon.

Make time each day

The manager should devote time each day to a specific project. Every day, you will be aware of what you should be doing. Disciplining yourself to doing the work is the key to putting a stop to your procrastination.

Do not tolerate distractions

Being aware of the effect the office can have on your productivity is important. An office that is too warm or cold can affect your rate of work. Draughts, noise and other pressures can reduce your capacity for concentration, so often an essential element in breaking out of procrastination. Don't tolerate distractions. Create the environment in which you can produce your best.

'To do' list

Don't let the amount of the day's work distract you from your 'must', 'should' and 'like' list. Ensure that you keep this with you at all times; otherwise you may be distracted.

Planning

Planning and preparation reduce the chances of things going wrong. When planning, don't forget to include the time frame and ensure that it is possible to achieve the deadlines within that time. Time can pressurize us and create much larger procrastination problems. It is therefore important to attend to the following points.

- When planning think about all aspects of the project.
- Can you delegate any of the work?
- What action can you take?
- Who will do it and when?

Often we re-invent the wheel because we feel that we have to complete all the work ourselves.

Procrastination can cost a great deal to the company, and the employee. The company is not enjoying the full potential of the staff, and the employee creates a number of problems for himself. These problems can grow out of all proportion, swamp the employee, and kill any career progression.

Chapter 7

Assertiveness . . . learning to say no!

How often have you been disturbed whilst working on an important project? How often has somebody successfully distracted you from important work and directed you to the urgent? How frequently do you feel that your tasks are put to one side because others interrupt and cause you to consider other courses of action? This may happen a great deal, but when it distracts you from completing work that is high priority, and focuses your attention on the work of others, it can create real problems.

Managers often find that they have to drop work on their key results areas because staff eat into their time and take them away from their objectives. In some cases, this means that they are living their working life according to the priorities of others. Although many feel that they should be more assertive and say no, they have difficulty in expressing their true feelings in a positive and assertive manner.

What is assertiveness?

Assertiveness is a skill which very few people possess. Assertiveness is the ability to express your true feelings in a positive manner without feeling guilty or being aggressive! Being assertive is a strategy which people adopt in order to avoid the violation of their rights and to ensure that others do not eat too much into their time! It is an extremely important skill. Some managers feel that, however well they structure their day, others will interrupt and their carefully planned programme will be deviated from in order to meet the requirements and priorities of others.

We have to expect some interruption, especially from our senior colleagues, our boss and those who work directly for us, but when we find that the influence of others directs us to do things 'that others are paid to do' then it is time that we took the necessary action.

Assertiveness is about changing the *actions, behaviour and attitudes* of others. Although attitude change is difficult to bring about in the short term, it is possible to influence others and make them change their behaviour, and the way they respond and act towards you. They must be made to realize that, in some circumstances, their actions can impact negatively on you. This can happen in many different ways. Using persuasive techniques, staff can manipulate and control *your* work behaviour and actions to fulfil *their* needs, at the expense of yours! There is nothing inherently wrong with this, except that, in these circumstances, your goals and objectives are sacrificed in order that their can be achieved. When this becomes a way of life for you, you seriously have to consider taking preventative action to avoid a recurrence.

How assertive are you?

Think through the various social and business situations in which you find yourself, and consider the degree to which you project your true feelings without embarrassment or guilt.

- At work, do you find that others can manipulate you to achieve their own ends?
- If someone annoys or upsets you, do you distance yourself from the situation and complain later to your colleagues and friends?
- How often do you find that you are 'over-burdened' with tasks you did not want to do, but, nevertheless, find yourself doing?
- Do you find it difficult to stand up to others when you disagree with them?
- Do you avoid confronting people because you fear the repercussions?
- Do you avoid telling others what you feel because you believe this would be personally upsetting or embarrassing?
- Do you spend too much time giving others 'subtle' hints rather than being direct with them?
- Do you let the work group significantly influence your actions and behaviour?
- How frequently do you say to yourself, 'If only I had said . . .'?

These are just some of the symptoms of not being sufficiently assertive to be able to cope with *your* time and *your* life. If you fail to take appropriate action you will find that less and less of the tasks you complete and the time you use will be directly related to meeting *your* key results areas.

Finally, when the manager decides to take some form of action, he worries about the impact of what he has to say. Could the expression of his true feelings alienate and antagonize his colleague? How will the latter react? Will he take the comments on board or shrug them aside and continue behaving in his same old way?

Awareness

We have assumed that managers recognize that time is being 'stolen' from them by those who interrupt and distract them from their work. But in some circumstances it is not always obvious. Sometimes, they are not aware that time is being stolen. This can happen in many different ways.

The organization drifter

The organization drifter is a case in point. How often have you settled down to get on with some really important work, only to have someone stop by your desk and take your attention? Colleagues or friends may start off by talking about their work, but deviate to talking about their weekend break, or their new house. Because of courtesy and custom, you engage in social conversation, but how do you end the conversation? When does the five minute break become ten, twenty, thirty minutes and, consequently, become a threat to your time management?

However well you plan the day, you must take account of contingencies. The short five-minute break spent being sociable can soon turn into a major time management problem. Where do you draw the line between valid and invalid reasons for conversation?

If you consider the most recent occasion when someone has stopped by, you will notice that once they have settled into their 'social space', it is very difficult to move them on. They have disturbed you at work, and if you fail to take action, you have complied with their wishes and created your own time waster!

Suddenly, you realize that your time is being eaten into and that you have to take some form of action. What do you say? You cannot be rude and dismiss your colleague for fear of giving offence. You will have to be tactful in trying to draw the conversation to a close. But what happens if you cannot do this? How do you convey the message that you wish to get on with your work?

It is not easy. You have to develop a number of strategies that will enable you, first of all, to placate the needs of the interrupter, and secondly, inform him that you do have work to complete.

Some managers find this problem very difficult to deal with. It is even more difficult if the chap who interrupts is your boss!

Office design

Office layout can encourage staff at all levels to become drifters. I can give one example, an insurance office, where the layout of the office influenced productivity. The office was open plan, and not designed with individual work stations and productivity in mind. The main consideration was 'getting as many desks as possible' into the space available. Little thought was given to segregating work stations, to traffic flow, or to separating functions. More staff were moved into the office, because of business expansion, and the department started to experience severe time management problems. Staff drifted, stopping at each other's desks for a quick chat. Management did not realize that a subject as simple as layout and accommodation was having such an impact on productivity.

After an investigation of the problem, it was suggested that the office layout be redesigned to provide separate work stations and greater privacy. In a relatively short time, a marked improvement in productivity was noted.

The physical surroundings can influence the circumstances which promote 'drifting'. If staff find it difficult to avoid or deflect unwanted attention, or use it as an excuse for procrastination, the individual work rate will fall drastically.

The telephone terror

Managers feel that the most difficult problem they face is signalling to the 'drifter' that it is time to go. You can do it if you are able to reinforce your message with non-verbal cues, body posture and words, but what happens when the person distracting you from the important work is a telephone caller?

You have only your social and interpersonal skills to rely on. You are forced to phrase a response that will not offend, and with which you will feel comfortable. Many give in. They recognize that they do not possess the skills and knowledge to express themselves honestly and truthfully, and they 'put up' with the consequences.

What are the consequences?

These are many and varied, but they all have one thing in common, they divert you from your course of action, and, if taken to the extreme, they can create a great deal of stress and anxiety for you! This happens quite simply by your 'giving in' to the time waster and then trying to achieve all you have set out for the day in a shorter time period. We know that 'work expands to fill the time available' but if you have planned your day reasonably well, using the daily planner, you may find that constant interruptions do turn a day devoted to results into a day of waste, characterized by chaos.

Eric Webster, in his book *How to Win the Business Battle*, discusses this point and says that 'Research suggests that the typical senior manager has only one hour alone each day, being interrupted every eight minutes, usually by subordinates seeking advice and information'.

No statistics as yet exist for other levels of management, but one can be sure that these problems permeate the whole organizational structure. The important point to note is that, although our attention may be focused by our boss, we still fall prey to those in the company who seek our help, guidance and approval, in other words, our staff. In fact, anyone can divert us from our chosen path, so we have to develop a balanced approach to time management, and build into our day some element of flexibility. But does this mean that we have to react at all times to the unexpected or the latest crisis, or does it mean that we have to become more assertive?

If we find that others are occupying our time and space unnecessarily, we must become committed to doing something about it. Where do we start?

Actions and behaviour

The tactics we adopt must lead to some form of behaviour modification. We have to change the way we respond to others in order to influence them. We can react in a number of ways to situations where we wish to express our true feelings, yet fail to do so.

Aggression

Those who feel most pressured will eventually 'crack' and 'blow up' verbally. This thoughtless reaction will then invoke more guilt than if the person had, at the outset, simply learned to say 'No I cannot help – I need to get on with this project'.

Exploding, and damaging a close working relationship, is not the best way of asserting yourself! Many equate aggression with assertion. They are wrong. They are confusing the use of *power* with that of *reason*.

Avoidance

Some adopt the passive approach and avoid taking any action but simply *hope* that things will change. Instead of creating change, they avoid situations which will lead to taking on more work or being distracted from their own path. Avoidance does not remedy the cause, but only covers up the symptoms of the problem. These people avoid taking the necessary action because they fear the reaction of others!

Accommodation

Accommodation is a strategy of living with the consequences. People whinge about accommodating the needs of others, but do nothing to reduce the impact of others on their results, because they are not prepared to take responsibility to eradicate the cause of the trouble.

Psychological space

To ensure that we solve the problem once and for all, we have to be prepared to learn the skills of assertiveness, thus rejecting the negative, aggressive approach, and the passivity of avoidance and accommodation.

Our psychological space is 'crowded' when we feel that others are critical of our values, beliefs, thoughts and feelings. These can also be threatened when others consume our time and deflect our attention from those things that we believe to be important. If others have little regard for our feelings, and damage our self-worth, we may wish to be assertive, but actually respond in other ways, i.e. avoid contact with them or the subject-matter, accommodate the intrusion or respond aggressively to it. These three approaches are negative, and do little to remedy the situation. Assertiveness is a rational approach to solving the problem without generating aggression in ourselves and others, and guilt or fear of retribution in ourselves.

Behaviour modification

Behaviour modification is the key to becoming more assertive. We first have to develop the will, the commitment and the motivation to do something about our apparent lack of assertion. Secondly, we have to be prepared to adopt behaviours we have never used before, and be prepared to improve our skills. Skill development does not take place in a vacuum. Skills cannot be acquired through reading and academic pursuits, they require practice in order to be reinforced and improved.

This need for practice deters many from trying new techniques, but it is the only foolproof method for acquiring assertiveness. The key to practice is preparation and planning. Thinking through the major issues, and planning our tactics, will remove some of the risk and anxiety from the situation.

Risk and anxiety may at first hold you back, but you must realize that practising your skills will provide you with the confidence you need to change *your* managerial behaviour so as to influence others!

We shape behaviour in a number of ways. An example to illustrate behavioural change relates to the teaching of children. If they do something that we encourage and support we should reward their behaviour in a positive manner. We may reinforce it by telling them that they are good and clever boys or girls. We are in the process of shaping self-esteem and worth. If on the other hand, we criticize them, the consequences will be that their self-worth will be low and that they believe themselves to be of little value!

Shaping behaviour through negative reinforcement *may* be effective when keeping children away from danger, but should *never* be used as the only method for learning. Children who develop, grow and feel good about themselves and their self-worth, are those with enquiring minds who are seeking positive 'strokes', and expect approval from others.

In a similar fashion, managers can shape the behaviour of the people with whom they work. They can reinforce certain behaviours, e.g. agreeing to take on work, but 'bitching' about it afterwards to

If you have failed to express your true feelings, how can you blame someone for asking for more of your time and your help? Continually taking on more than you can handle, and resenting it in the process, can seriously affect your effectiveness and your health. If you fail to communicate your true feelings, can you really expect others to understand how you feel?

Insensitivity

Because of the tensions and demands of business, we tend to overlook certain problems. Targets are agreed, and we work feverishly towards them, constantly aware of the fear of failing to meet our goals. Those who are time pressured and have results to achieve can tend to become very task orientated. In other words, we tend to forget about the 'people' side of the operation. Instead, we tend to become target centred. We may, at the same time, avoid or misread the feelings of others.

We may also not be prepared to express our thoughts, and become more assertive in communicating our feelings and thoughts. It is not therefore surprising that the behaviour of others does not change. They are not mind-readers!

Managers' responsibility

I have spoken to many managers about their assertiveness problems and find that too many project their feelings and blame colleagues. I have to tell them that they hold the responsibility for themselves and for the way they behave.

Negative impact

For instance, a person I know became very negative about his boss, and spent much of his time complaining about him to others. He became tense and strained. He did not get too much fun out of work. He created his own negative spiral. At the end of the day he took his problems home to his wife. He made her unhappy. To break out of the negative spiral he has had to force himself to take responsibility for his own future, and become more assertive.

Saying 'no'!

Simply saying 'no' is not sufficient to discourage others from eating into your time. You have to say it with conviction and be prepared to hold your ground. To illustrate this point, I recently had to replace a photocopier for my office. I had made a number of enquiries and visits to various office equipment suppliers. One persistent young man was very keen for me to buy from him. He phoned me at the office at all times of the day. I told him I had not yet made up my mind and that I would contact him in the near future when I had made my decision. After that, he phoned again. I told him that I had decided to go to a competitor. In a last ditch attempt to get the sale, he tried to project guilt onto me, by saying how much time he had spent on my needs, the constant phone calls, etc. He finally asked, in an attempt to discredit his competitor, and perhaps win back the sale, which machine I had bought and from whom I had bought it. I told him that I had made my decision, that I was thankful for his help and that I hoped to make use of his company some time in the future. He would not give up. He tried to direct me back to the sale and my reasons for purchase. He was now firing on all cylinders and obviously needed his commission!

I asserted myself. 'Thank you for your help. I see little point discussing my purchase with you, as I have made a decision based upon my needs. If I need any further advice, information or equipment I will bear your company in mind. Thank you for phoning, I must get back to my work now. Goodbye.'

Tactics to get you to say 'yes'

Although the above is not a classic case in 'assertiveness', the transaction possessed all the ingredients. The salesman tried to trade on my guilt for eating into his time. He tried to create a situation in which the customer 'felt guilty for not buying'. Thankfully, this does not happen too frequently in the commercial world, but I am sure you can think of instances when you have been made to feel uncomfortable for saying 'no'.

A further example occurred when friends of mine visited a 'time-share location'. The invitation to visit stated that no obligation was attached to it. However, the sales staff were very insistent, and developed the climate in which people felt guilty for taking up their time. I heard later that this technique had done a great deal to get people to sign there and then, but a large number of people returned later to 'change their minds'. The situation, and the pressure generated by the sales team had done a great deal to create tension and reinforce the feeling of guilt for taking up time but not buying the product.

Many consumers are 'blackmailed' into buying things they don't want because of pressurized guilt. Once you are aware of the technique, you can resist it by simply saying *no*! Many salesmen try to get you to explain your reasoning, and try to establish your objections so that they can come back with a 'benefits package'. Do not fall for it. Say 'no'. You should not feel obliged to give a reason, although you may be pushed for one. It may make you feel uncomfortable, but say 'no' and thus avoid buying what you do not want!

This same technique can be cunningly applied by your colleagues, and your boss! They can use guilt to get you to do things you do not want to do. They may put you in a difficult situation and rely on guilt to try to make you change your mind. You have to resist this and may wish to state the reason why you cannot help by giving a personal reason or one relating to the consequences of not doing what you plan to do. For example:

'I cannot work on the report at the weekend, I have long-standing plans to see my daughter's graduation.'

If your colleague then tells you that he thinks you have your priorities wrong, and 'the company needs your help now', you must continue your assertive message. 'Yes, I understand the problem, but I booked for this weekend some time ago. It is not my fault that the report has only just come to the company's notice.'

Your 'opponent' may then mix guilt with an appeal to your sympathy, and use complimentary behaviour: 'Look, you know how important this is. We really do need your help. We can't do it by ourselves, and you have the skills. Think about the difficulty we will have working without your expertise'.

You reply: 'Yes, I understand your difficulties, and you may think I am selfish putting my trip before company business, but, as I said before, this has been booked for some time. Besides, this report was really the responsibility of others. I shall be going away at five tonight'.

A strategy to get off the hook is to help the person urging you to do something to take action himself which will help him achieve his goal. You could either suggest the names of others who could help, or make available some time in the future (e.g. Monday a.m.) for a brief discussion. The major point is that you are determined to have your 'weekend away' but you are willing to offer advice and information that may help in setting up alternative arrangements.

Many fall for the guilt routine. Lack of assertion contributes not just to taking on extra work, but to other issues such as, for example, giving a colleague a lift in your car when you really wanted to say 'no' because it was taking you out of your way, and forcing you to be late home. A great deal of stress is created every day by people saying 'yes', when they want to say 'no'.

Use of authority

People in positions of authority can create a radical change in behaviour in others for a host of reasons. Deciding to say 'no' to your boss is one which could influence your whole career, but the point to note is that your *boss* can be your biggest time waster! He may be an excellent manager in delegating most of his tasks to others, and spending a great deal of his available time thinking through strategic issues, but you must assess how his style affects *your* effectiveness!

To assert your rights regarding your major work duties and your time you have to choose whether to tolerate the present situation, or take some action and become more effective in your work.

Milgram and the power of the situation

You must be aware of other problems which managers face related to authority, many of which are examined in Milgram's research into power and authority. Stanley Milgram conducted over a thousand experiments with adult subjects, who were picked from varied social and professional backgrounds. The experiment was conducted by an experimenter, a naive partner (teacher) and an accomplice (learner). The experimenter explained that the experiment would consist of a number of roles to be played. The 'naive' subject was not aware that the experiments and the roles were 'rigged'.

The naive subject always occupied the position of 'teacher' and the accomplice was the 'learner'. The experiment was, supposedly, to test the effect of punishment on memory. In effect it was concerned with examining the use and influence of authority in certain situations.

The experiment required the 'teacher' to ask questions of the 'learner'. The 'teacher' and 'learner' were positioned in separate rooms. The learner was wired up to an electric shock generator, which was fake.

If the learner failed to answer the questions from the 'teacher' correctly, the teacher administered a slight (fake) electric shock. The 'teacher' could see the 'learner' through a glass partition. The 'learner' was a good actor, and always faked the screams when the 'teacher' thought he was administering the shock.

The teacher, under the careful supervision of the experimenter, had control of the shock generator which was clearly marked from 15 to 450 volts. Although a fake generator, the 'teacher' was not aware that the shocks he was administering were fake.

To add to the reality of the situation, the teacher could hear the 'anguished screams' of the learner. The 'teacher's role' was to ask set questions and, if the learner got them wrong, the 'teacher' had to administer the punishment, i.e. electric shocks. The 'teacher' had to increase progressively the power of the shocks, even if the 'learner' would not respond.

Shocked by their conformity

Many who took part in the experiment were 'shocked' by their behaviour during it. Why? Up to two-thirds of those playing 'teacher' were pushed to go to the maximum voltage. Although the 'learner's' screams got louder and louder, the teacher obeyed instructions. When, as on occasions, the teacher started to panic, or refused to continue the experiment because the screams were becoming too intense, the experimenter, who was standing overlooking the experiment, pressed the teacher to go on! 'The experiment requires that you continue.'

One-third did not obey, but the majority bent to authority. Why did they obey, when they thought that the 'learner', a man in the street who like the teacher had been asked to take part in the experiment, was experiencing a great deal of pain?

The implications

Milgram's research has some frightening implications for the control and influence of people. It points to situational factors influencing the actions and behaviours of people. However assertive we think we are, there are always times and situations where our will can be influenced, and can force us to do things that we would not normally do.

Milgram suggests that this may have accounted for the 'submission of prisoners', who willingly walked to concentration camps, although they knew their fate, and the atrocities of My Lai in Vietnam. What other atrocities will man be forced to commit because he does not possess the strength of power to go against authority or group opinion? Milgram states, 'It is not so much the type of person a man is, as the kind of situation in which he finds himself.' Clearly, his research suggests that, in many circumstances, man is prepared to bend to authority.

Relating this research to the workplace is interesting, because it forces us to think about the situations where we have or do not have sufficient power, influence or persuasive skills to resist authority, or situations where we have little *perceived* control.

Zimbardo and others have looked at similar experiments in different contexts, and their conclusions suggest that man is ready to 'conform' in many social situations. Sceptics suggest that it was the artificiality of the experiments that created the 'conformity' and that man would not conform to the same degree in organizational life. But consider the following: the experimenter's power was vested in a white lab coat and the simple speech, 'The experiment requires that you continue administering the punishment'.

At work, authority is rigid and the sanctions that can be applied are more powerful than those in experimental conditions. Is it any wonder that so many of us need to become more assertive?

What to do

Structure your time

Consider the impact of others on the management of your time. Are you convinced that you have sufficient control over your time or does it belong to others? Be prepared to accept that your boss and the system impose tasks upon you that require you to structure your time in order to leave as much as possible for the tasks we can class as 'self-imposed'.

Many try to project the 'macho' image and pretend that they are assertive. You will be surprised at the number of tasks we do each day because we don't have the confidence or the skills to state our true feelings.

Repetition

On a simple level, repetition is an excellent method for 'telling it how it is'. When asked to do work or spend time on things which are outside your responsibility, it is necessary, on occasions, to state the obvious more than once! Saying 'no' once, may not work. Those who want you to do something are either going to rephrase their statement in a number of ways or repeat themselves. They could adopt the strategy of wearing you down during the day, but you should be resolute and remember to rephrase the content of your message.

For the long-term issue, for instance, your boss wanting you to take a new responsibility which you are far from happy about, will require different skills from those required by the problem above. You will require resilience and stamina and must refuse to enter the debate of explanations.

The repetitive approach is particularly useful on the phone. Restatements of a phrase which reflects the same sentiment will eventually work.

'Well, I agree my attitude may appear negative, but there is no way I can help you. I have explained that I have made other commitments, and changing them would create a great deal of personal problems for myself.'

What this approach requires is that you listen and rephrase what the person on the phone says. You do not argue, you respond sensibly and rationally. You must not be dragged into 'emotion', you must remain in the world of fact.

You can use another, similar style: 'Yes, I recognize that I may have created some problems for you, and that you feel I owe it to the company to spend the weekend on the report, but I did explain the reason for my weekend away, and while I agree that it may be inconvenient for the company, the consequences of not seeing my daughter's graduation would cause me great upset'.

Listening

Clearly, the skills you need to develop are interpersonal in nature. The ability to listen attentively to what is said, what is not said and what can't be said without help, is the key to active listening. We spend little time developing the skill of listening. We tend to assume that listening is easy, a passive process. It is not.

Becoming a keen, critical and active listener requires a great deal of effort. We can become better listeners by not confusing the important message with the one that interests us. Sometimes we become selective and only listen to 'what we want to hear'. We can miss many cues, which later may become more overt statements. A good listener sifts, screens and hunts for relevant information.

Use your time positively, structuring and restructuring your thoughts. Do not evade what you consider to be the difficult message. Managers can give in to requests, not because they think they ought, but because they lose the physical battle. They stop listening and surrender.

Perhaps the most important part of listening for the manager who wants to avoid being overloaded is 'reflective listening'. This technique is based on non-directive interviewing and counselling, and requires you to reflect the words back to the 'sender of the request' in a different format, but not adding, subtracting or introducing emotion, feelings or value statements.

'Well, John, I'm not too happy about your weekend trip to London. It really is going to create all sorts of problems for us. We don't know when we are going to finish the report. Can't you reconsider the trip? Let me have a word with your wife, I'm sure she will understand.'

How should you respond . . .?

'Paul, you know my position on this. I do understand that you will have difficulty finishing off the report, and that you will have to come to terms with some problems, but I have given you the reason for my trip, and explained the consequences of not going. I understand you would like to talk to Helen, my wife, but I must tell you that we are determined to go to London to see my daughter graduate from university.'

Silence

The non-directive or reflective listening technique is useful if you apply the silence rule. Many managers find it very difficult not to start talking if silences occur in a conversation. If silence persists for six to eight seconds they are inclined to jump in to break it. You must learn to use silence. State your view and then shut up. There is nothing more to say. If your opponent speaks up again, just restate your comments and then keep quiet. There is no need to say more! Silence is probably the best friend to someone who is keen to eradicate the impositions of others.

Focus on solutions

Let us consider that while you are being assertive you also wish to be fairly constructive and positive. It is not as easy as it sounds. If you have not tried the technique before, you could end up giving in, or just delaying the time when you will start the work or tasks of others.

The point to note here is that after saying 'no', you can provide the interrupter with some information which will help him achieve his goal. He may not be too pleased that you have rejected his proposals but he will be grateful that you have helped him consider alternative arrangements.

Preparation

As with all things, we reduce the risks of failure by realistically planning ahead. Spending time on planning and preparation helps us identify the sort of message we want to send, and helps us highlight the important aspects of the message. Preparing for an encounter can be false because we pick up so much work every day, simply by lifting the phone. We have to learn to be more direct and think through our objections to others. This means we may wish to examine 'excuses' that we can use. This can be a dangerous stance, because we can add too much information to the message and be dragged into debating the pros and cons. Beware of using excuses.

When planning, don't expect that everything you say has to be sound sensible stuff. You may adopt the approach where you say, 'You may be right, only time will tell, but you know my position and I must make the trip to London'. Here you are not saying that your colleague or boss is wrong. You are not antagonizing his views, only communicating that you will not be able to meet his requirements this time.

Remember not to confuse aggression with assertion, and do move away from the passive approach of avoidance and accommodation.

You will find plenty of time to practise your new skills. You are not yet aware how much time you spend doing the work of others. In some instances, this work may be legitimate, but in many circumstances people take on work because they do not know how to say 'no' without feeling guilty and fearing the consequences.

Chapter 8

Making meetings work: the structure

Meetings can occupy a great deal of every manager's time. They can be the key to effective communication, problem solving, and decision making, but, in many instances, can consume too much time.

Consider the last time you attended a meeting, and ask yourself whether the quality of the decisions reached was of value to the company. How often do we find that the cost of holding and attending a meeting far exceeds the financial value of the decisions agreed? The financial costs of meetings can be staggering. Work out the costs of attendance, and double it. What could the manager be doing instead? Every choice has an opportunity cost. In this case, it means the manager could be devoting his time to revenue generating activities, rather than consuming time and contributing little. Meetings should be made to be cost effective.

If you recognize these symptoms as a common occurrence in your organization, you should spend time analysing and eradicating the cause of the problem.

What is a meeting?

A meeting is an opportunity for a number of managers to get together to solve a common problem. Meetings should be gatherings where quality decisions are made, by using information and debate to agree a course of action. Meetings should be a forum for lively questioning and opportunities to test and develop new ideas. They should be positive, stimulating forums of debate.

Let's not assume that all managers attend the same variety and level of meeting. Clearly, the organization, its size, the technology employed, and the service or goods supplied, will have some effect upon the type of meetings held.

In a company that is experiencing fierce competition with a number of different products with short product life cycles, the meeting may be an essential method of disseminating information amongst the management team. The content, structure and organization of meetings may well be affected by whether the organization is in the private or the public sector.

Local authorities may have a complicated committee structure that requires constant meetings and feedback to various bodies. The nature of decision making in the public sector tends to be based upon 'consensus', and requires information to be communicated to a variety of groups. The requirement that some decisions should reflect consensus of all groups concerned, itself stultifies and slows down the decision-making process. Meetings can be long drawn out affairs that require small *ad hoc* working parties to report back, and this can further reduce their effectiveness.

Formal and informal

Meetings can be classed as formal or informal. Those in the public domain require adherence to a precise code of conduct that has been designed to reduce time. But informal meetings can occupy a great deal of a manager's time. His progress may, in some circumstances, be determined by his ability to group staff together to discuss a problem of immediate consequence. Informal meetings can take up far more time than formal ones. In some cases, this is where the greatest amount of time wasting occurs.

Poor image

Meetings have gained a poor image as a method of decision making. Many managers recognize that the meetings they attend are a 'waste of time'. They complain that their attendance cuts down their effectiveness. Meetings, in effect, can be classed as dead time. But is this true for all meetings in all organizations? Clearly not.

In many organizations, the manager's effectiveness would be reduced significantly if the time spent at meetings were reduced. These organizations value the opportunity to test and develop new solutions to problems. They recognize that the purpose of meetings is to exchange information and make decisions about the problems that exist.

Time wasters

Meetings themselves are not time wasters, but those who attend can create the circumstances by which meetings get a poor name. What are these circumstances? What can be done to develop meetings into forums for effective decision making?

There are two interrelated areas that need to be investigated when converting the poor to an effective meeting. These are:

- *Structure and content.* How meetings are organized and structured, and how time is allocated to business at hand.
- *Process and behaviour.* The quality of contribution and the 'how' of decision making.

Structure and content

There are many negative elements associated with the structural characteristics of meetings. Meetings can be attended for a whole host of reasons. When questioned, managers say they need to attend all meetings to retain their knowledge of what is going on in the organization. Many recognize the importance of keeping up to date and acquiring information that will be of direct use in their job. But does this compensate for the potential time which can be wasted? No.

Many managers confuse attendance at meetings with performance. This is certainly the case as they rise up the hierarchy. Many of them are invited to attend more out of courtesy than need. Unfortunately, they do not recognize the problem until it has become a 'way of life' for them. They do not evaluate the reasons for attendance. They think that 'attendance' is an essential aspect of their job.

At the end of the week, a manager may have spent 20% of his time at meetings of one form or another, but find that only 3% of this time was well spent. It is clear that he will have to be more selective and choose to go to the meetings which will have the payoffs he requires.

Responsibilities of the chairman

Undoubtedly, the responsibility for effective meetings rests with the chairman, but to what extent does he possess the knowledge and the experience to do a good job?

We tend to assume that managers develop their ability to run meetings as they progress in their career. There are very few opportunities to develop this expertise except by 'sitting next to Nellie'. This is not the best training.

Some managers seem to be 'born chairmen'. But others take time to ease into the role. How many over-long, poorly directed meetings does it take before the chairman is sufficiently skilled, experienced, and confident to deal with business in a proficient manner? We pay the cost of training by default. His experience is gained at our expense.

Most meetings require a confident chairman who is trained, not only in procedure, but also in helping others express themselves. Many forget the importance of the 'facilitating role'. They forget that the chairman's role is to establish a method for solving the problems under discussion. This requires drawing on the experience and talents of those present, and helping others to understand things from different perspectives.

The role of the chairman is partly educative. He is required to listen to what others say, what they don't say, and what they cannot say without help. His purpose in doing this is to ensure that decisions are made by consensus. This means asking for opinions, expressing complex ideas and statements in the most simple form, and ensuring that those who do not usually contribute, have sufficient opportunity to express their intentions, feelings and thoughts in a positive climate.

The 80/20 rule

Although a great deal of work and discussion in committees or meetings borders on 'politicking', the role of the chairman is to ensure that everybody has a chance to debate issues that are pertinent to the problem under discussion.

He must ensure that everybody has his say. He must ensure that the 'minority' do not control and influence the proceedings. In a large meeting, it is usual for a minority of those present to influence significantly the content of the decisions reached. This is the 80/20 rule drawn from the statistician, Vilfredo Pareto.

The Pareto Principle can be applied to management problems. In the case of meetings, the 80/20 rule suggests that 80% of the contribution comes from 20% of those attending. It is not important that the percentages are exact, rather that generally the rule holds true, especially in larger meetings.

The 80/20 rule also applies to telephone calls, customer sales, administration and paperwork, i.e. 80% of a company's telephone calls are made to 20% of their customers or suppliers; 80% of company revenue comes from 20% of the customer base; and 80% of paperwork demands emanate from 20% of managers.

The rule proves true in many circumstances, both social and business. The important point to note is that the chairman of the meeting must ensure that full discussion has taken place and not let the 20% of the major contributors hog the floor.

Fear of looking a fool and the comfort of conformity

It is imperative that all present who have something to say have the opportunity to express their ideas. The chairman should ensure this by generating an environment where managers feel they can contribute without looking a fool.

Fear of appearing foolish can be the biggest problem experienced by individual managers in meetings. This is especially true of younger managers in large meetings. They are aware that their behaviour and contribution will be judged and evaluated, so they don't 'bounce' around good ideas. They are also fearful of saying the 'wrong things' and, on occasion, avoid saying anything that can be construed as challenging the status quo. They constantly look for signals that reflect 'what is acceptable' and spend too much time managing their image, rather than managing the quality of decisions.

Instead of being innovative and creative, many new managers and those who wish to rise quickly stick to the same outmoded behaviour as their more successful counterparts and seniors, and do not come up with any new ideas. This fear of looking foolish can breed the wrong type of managerial style. Younger managers, especially new graduates, are always on the lookout for 'hints' or indicators of what is expected of them.

Politics

Meetings are the perfect forum for watching the 'hawks and vultures' gather. Managers who have, or who have not, made their mark over the years, will be keen to present their views.

The politics associated with managing and contributing to meetings in some of our larger institutions are far less important than the decisions reached. Unfortunately, they seem to occupy too much time and the importance given to these events borders on the absurd.

For the manager who is keen to progress up the ladder, it is best to avoid the politics of becoming too involved in meetings. A point can be scored here and there but people have long memories, and I wonder if the disproportionate time we spend in the 'political arena' has any impact on achieving results and promoting effectiveness. I doubt it. What we are concerned with promoting is the 'quest for achieving results'.

Commitment

The chairman has to be committed to making things work. He must be committed to ensuring that the tasks or issues in front of the meeting are debated thoroughly and that the due structure and formality of the meeting is observed. However, this can be taken to extremes.

The mechanics of 'proposing, seconding and voting' can be taken out of all proportion to the content and importance of the issues under discussion. Here, the chairmen involved rely heavily on the book of rules. This, in their view, separates the good chairman from the poor. They are wrong! At the end of the day, the spirit and the intent of the discussion mirrored in short, but illustrative and comprehensive, minutes, is more important than the constitutional rigours that have been applied!

One should not forget the constitution and procedures, but there must be balance. Of course, we should ensure that quorums and points of order are understood and applied, but, in many circumstances, the formality of the meeting, perhaps a long-standing committee, has blocked any meaningful discussion, rapport and problem solving.

It is clear that the chairman should be committed to ensuring that all items on the agenda are discussed in order to arrive at meaningful and appropriate action. Some areas of his responsibilities are task orientated and others are related to people. This can be demonstrated first by looking at the alternative management styles that the chairman can take.

He may adopt an authoritarian style and be extremely directive. Although business may be agreed, can we be sure that all members will really feel they are committed to action which has been structured under the directive eye of an autocratic chairman? Conversely, the chairman could spend all his time pleasing the immediate needs of those attending, devoting a disproportionate time to facilitating their needs rather than dealing with the business on hand. The worst style is that of the 'abdicator'. This chap has little commitment to the task or the people attending. He merely 'muddles through' and adheres to the rules and procedures. Beyond this, his effectiveness is low.

Obviously, a matter of balance is required so that chairmen feel they have achieved results through the involvement and participation of those attending. When the chairman moves from the ideal type or 'balance' we should ensure that the whole meeting is not run or managed in an unbalanced way.

The longest agenda

Many of you will not be surprised to hear of the 'case of the longest agenda'. This was presented at a faculty board of a business school. Here, the business of the board was to discuss the provision of courses throughout a large college. The agenda covered two sides of A4 paper and each line was fully used. In addition, there were numerous papers attached for discussion. The majority of these had been circulated prior to the meeting, but many were tabled. There were over twenty-six papers! The situation was clearly chaotic but still the meeting went ahead.

The quality of the decisions reached was called into question. Many staff, when receiving their pre-meeting papers, decided not to go. Others attended only for a short time, keeping a public profile with their heads of department, but neglecting the issues at hand. They recognized that *attendance* was more important than *performance*.

How could the business for the day be achieved in such circumstances? It was not. Participants tried to cover too much business in too little time. Each issue had to be debated at length. There was little attempt to summarize. Business was conducted in no apparent order of priority. The method of dealing with issues had been fixed twenty years ago, and the same format had persisted to the present, when the college was running more courses and had greater resources to call upon.

Poor management of meetings is not solely the province of education establishments. It is also found in the public sector and private companies. We can all quote instances where business was impeded by factors caused by the poor structure and content of the meeting.

Action to improve meetings

Agenda

The agenda is the structure of the meeting, the framework through which decisions are reached. In many instances, the agenda does not facilitate the business of the meeting at all. On analysis, the agenda may be a hotchpotch of items arranged in no apparent order of priority.

Consequently, at the end of a meeting we may find that the items which did not merit lengthy debate and consideration have taken up far too much time. Usually this happens at the expense of other items which did require thorough debate and analysis.

Failing to classify and prioritize items can create situations where meetings may be held, but the decisions reached have little impact on key result areas.

Agendas must be constructed around priorities. Some items which require less debate and discussion may be placed at the beginning of the session, but must not take over from the spirit of the meeting. Getting a sense of direction, and ensuring that the *high priority* items are dealt with in the proper fashion, is imperative. Clearly, the responsibility for direction rests with the chairman, but, if all else fails, others attending *must* take some responsibility for ensuring that work is dealt with in a swift and effective manner.

Taking responsibility

At the conclusion of a 'poor or ineffective' meeting we will always find the negative character who puts 100 per cent of the blame on the poor leadership offered by the chairman. If such a person is prepared to attend, participate in and 'put up with' such meetings, his behaviour can be rated on a par with that of the official chairman.

When those attending meetings recognize that things are not going well, they have a responsibility to improve matters. Although they cannot take over the session, they can take some form of action to ensure that the meeting does conform to some order.

Summarizing, or suggesting various courses of action, can help to direct the attention of attendees back on course. Adopting a blunt, 'It is not my responsibility' stance does little to promote the right attitude for achieving results.

All those attending sessions have a responsibility to themselves, their colleagues and, if appropriate, their constituents to ensure that business is dealt with in a professional manner. If it is not, they must shoulder some responsibility for the consequences.

Restructuring meetings

A company that recognized that meetings were a big time waster decided to restructure them. First, it ensured that all agenda items should be fixed. On no account should any agenda items be tabled. How an busy managers have the time and commitment to read through additional items and reach a good quality decision in those circumstances?

Items that are tabled for discussion can throw the main business of the agenda off course. If the item is so important, surely it warrants calling a meeting especially to cover it.

Deciding upon, and agreeing, a method for the inclusion of agenda items a day or two prior to the meeting is the only way of ensuring that other items are not introduced in an *ad hoc* manner.

Once the rule is adhered to, and never broken, managers will take time to organize and plan their time to ensure that agenda items reflect the business needs and issues that require to be discussed. The flexible alternative leads only to breakdown.

No 'any other business'

'Any other business' (AOB) can take up a disproportionate amount of time. This is the opportunity for managers to introduce red herrings or their favourite hobby horses. Avoid AOB, cancel it from the agenda, and make alternative arrangements to communicate and inform others of important developments. If items merit high priority they should be listed on the agenda, or dealt with in other appropriate ways.

Time limits

The company mentioned previously decided that meetings were generally too long. A meeting that started at 0930 would continue on to lunchtime. The same meeting if started an hour later would somehow still be concluded by lunch. Parkinson's Law seemed to override the objective of the meetings session.

'Work expands to fill the time available for its completion.'

The company decided to take preventative action and experimented with time limits. They decided that meetings should not last longer than one hour, the rationale being that most managers attending would have fallen off their learning curve, would not be listening to the content and intent of the sessions, and would agree to any course of action to bring the meetings to a close.

Immediately the company brought in the one-hour rule. They stated that on no account should a meeting last longer than 60 minutes. If a meeting were to last longer than that, it would indicate poor pre-meeting planning.

Items had not been discussed or even thought through before being placed on the agenda. If items did occupy a significant place in the strategic thrust of the company then surely they would deserve a well-prepared meeting.

What the company decided to do was to put the managers under pressure to think carefully through, work on, and debate the major cases, arguments or proposals prior to the session. Clearly, this would involve a great deal of pre-meeting planning and informal discussion, but it would ensure that all attending were fully conversant with the issues under debate.

The company also decided that the first item on the agenda would be planning and organizing the meeting. Members would agree, within fairly flexible guidelines, the structure, sequence and priority afforded to specific items. Time limits would be agreed within the flexible guidelines.

What one must be aware of when using the structured and time constrained agenda is that, from time to time, issues do emerge which require to be introduced at a meeting. Planning should be sufficiently flexible to allow the occasional introduction of the high priority issue, but if this becomes the norm, complete control of the meeting is lost.

Flexibility within structure is the key to success. Additional items should be introduced only if they fall within the following two categories: *emergency* or *strategic* issues.

Attendance

How often do meetings begin on time? If they do not, and those attending wait for others to arrive before starting business, the latecomers are penalizing those who do turn up on time.

Sooner or later, this group of managers will recognize that coming late is permissible and they will follow the examples of their tardy colleagues. The 2 p.m. meeting which doesn't start till 2.10 will soon become a way of life.

Those who do show up late and 'apologize' realize that business has not started so decide to come later in the day. Overall, the effect is devastating. Lateness becomes the norm and meetings start developing a reputation that they do not deserve.

We should all strive to achieve reinforcing behaviour. Starting on time penalizes the latecomer, and rewards the prompt attender. We should seek to use positive reinforcement to mould behaviour at meetings and begin on time.

Minutes

How often have you attended meetings and found your colleagues reading through the minutes of the previous meeting for the *first* time? There can be a number of reasons for this. Failing to distribute the minutes in adequate time can create difficulties, but the pure laziness of managers failing to read through the notes and official decisions and actions of previous meetings can also do much to waste valuable time.

The one liner!

Agreeing minutes can take up time that would be better used elsewhere. A popular but simple technique that can help to reduce the problems associated with writing and agreeing minutes is to summarize a decision in a brief note known as a 'one-liner'.

As the members of the meetings are coming to their conclusions a 'one line statement' is agreed which reflects the intent and content of the actions to be taken or decisions reached. This 'one liner' must typify the intent of the action and be the guiding statement for subsequent action. At further meetings, the 'one liner' can act as a good memory prompt to remind those attending what was actually agreed.

Having those attending the session agree on a quick 'one liner' before they move on to the next item on the agenda is the best way to avoid the disagreements which can often emerge when the 'minute writer' fails to cover everything in the minutes.

Agreeing to circulate minutes in a specified time can reduce a great deal of the conflict which can erupt at meetings when managers claim either that they had not received the minutes at all, or that they were received too late to consult before the meeting.

Pre-planning

For the really important meeting which may take place annually or bi-annually, it is worth while preparing for dealing with those items on the agenda that require rigorous analysis.

The items which need a thorough discussion are those which impact upon the effectiveness of the business. They may be related to an investment decision, a five-year plan, use of resources, a major reorganization, etc. These items require far more thought and discussion than others. It is clear that the chairman should have a clear idea of the causes and consequences of taking various actions.

He needs prior information so that he can conduct the meeting in a sensible and rigorous manner. He needs to be aware of all the arguments, and to perceive problems from different angles. The wise chairman will do some preliminary work and approach his colleagues to ascertain their views.

Doing this informally has little impact. People are willing to talk at length, and most of their discussion could be centred not necessarily on projecting a point of view, but rather on testing out their ideas. The chairman needs something that is a little more concrete and tangible.

The best approach is to circulate a document, called a *pre-meeting planner* (PMP) (see Fig. 8.1), to get a good idea of how people feel about a particular issue. The PMP should be distributed to all who are scheduled to attend the meeting session, completed and returned in time for collation and analysis.

This information forms the nucleus for discussion. Managers are requested to complete the PMP and identify:

- the problem, what it is and what it isn't, and how it affects them. The manager has the opportunity to state the nature of the problem and describe it in clear terms from his perspective;
- the probable causes of the problem, from the manager's viewpoint;
- possible solutions for the problem under investigation; and
- the most likely solution or the one which best meets the needs of the manager.

The idea behind the PMP is simple. It is well known that at large meetings the contribution from those attending tends to waver around the 20 per cent mark. Clearly, all opinions are never voiced, nor are they debated.

Too many ideas remain in the manager's mind!

Many good and valuable ideas stay in the minds of those attending. People do not come up with new, innovative solutions for fear of looking foolish. Formal meetings require all to contribute. Unfortunately, the size and the importance of these meetings creates the climate of 'conformity', and, consequently, no one comes up with new ideas.

The PMP avoids this. It helps those structuring the meeting to ensure that all points are addressed before a decision is reached. This approach avoids the 'quick fix' solution and encourages all to contribute.

However, there is a danger. Do not use the pre-meeting planner too often. Some chairmen have been known to use the document too freely. They have circulated a PMP for all items on the agenda! Guess what happened. No one returned the PMP!

Selectivity should be the watchword. Use of the PMP should be used only on *high priority* items, otherwise this device will soon become sucked into the old bureaucratic way of doing things.

Sub-committees and working parties

An unfortunate but necessary part of meetings is the use of sub-committees and working parties. They are necessary in circumstances that require professional people to examine a problem in depth, outside the meeting room.

Much of the work they do is developmental and research orientated. Committees are formed to address major problems and report back with conclusions. However, many of these groups earn themselves a poor reputation. Why?

The biggest problem they face is clarifying the work that is delegated to them. The main meeting might be unable to reach the right decision, so they procrastinate, form a working group to examine the alternatives, and thus delay a decision.

Meanwhile, those who have been unfortunate enough to have been selected for the task have to acquaint themselves quickly with the problem. If they fail to question, then and there, the expectations of the larger group and the parameters set, then they will fail in their task. They will fail because others have not supplied them with an accurate outline.

The working group is not supplied with all the information. It starts off disadvantaged. Members are unsure what the objectives of their work are. They are usually asked to report back on their findings.

It would appear that the larger group of managers have the faith to delegate the task to this smaller group, but have they obeyed the first law of delegation and defined the objectives in precise terms? Probably not!

PRE-MEETING PLANNER

You will shortly be attending the Company Strategic Planning session.
Because of the importance of item 3 on the agenda, office automation policy, we would like you to think through the main issues, read the enclosed documentation and complete this form, which should then be sent to Carl Edgar, the Chairman,
by (time) .... on (date)
....

STRATEGIC PLANNING GROUP   Date of Meeting ....

1. DISCUSSION ITEM

2. MAJOR CAUSE OF THE PROBLEM

3. POSSIBLE SOLUTIONS OR ACTION

4. THE OPTIMUM SOLUTION

  a. THE COSTS OF THIS APPROACH

  b. THE BENEFITS OF THIS APPROACH

Signature...Date ....

Instructions to working groups

- Ensure that the team picked has the necessary skills and experience to do a good job.
- Do not use this temporary group as a 'management development' exercise for younger managers. Many would class this as abdication of responsibility by senior staff which creates a climate for failure. It also creates the belief that 'younger managers' are associated with unpopular tasks.
- Be precise when defining terms of reference. If you genuinely don't know what they should do, tell them, but don't penalize them if their conclusions are poor!
- Ensure they are clear about your expectations. Set up review dates when they can report progress to the chairman.
- Ensure they have the resources and back-up to do a good job.
- Set a precise date for completion of the work. Specify the method and media that you wish the team to use. Do you want a management presentation or a report? If you want the latter, define the profile and the headings you would like discussed.

Remember, setting work to keep people busy is easy. What is difficult is achieving the desired results. So often with work delegated to working groups we find that it is lost forever, or conclusions and recommendations are presented which bear little relationship to the original problem.

Fig. 8.1 The pre-meeting planner

Chapter 9

Making meetings work: the process

The previous chapter outlined the formalism, the structure and discipline of meetings, but avoided the behavioural factors.

Many researchers have spent time watching, recording, and assessing the contribution which managers make to reaching decisions. They have examined the personal strategies that some managers use to get their own way. What follows is a constructive appraisal of the approach which some trainers use to improve the effectiveness of meetings.

Many have applied the work of Rackham and Carlisle *et al.* to the assessment of the styles which people use in meetings. This model is based upon the original idea of Bales.

The contribution which managers make in meetings determines the quality of decisions reached. We have already referred to the 80/20 rule. You will notice that as the size of a meeting increases from four to five managers to double figures and beyond, generally speaking, the majority of the contributions will come from a small number of those attending. The 80/20 rule holds well in most circumstances, and is certainly the case when meetings become even larger.

In large meetings many participants never actually contribute anything. The purpose of analysing the variety and length of the contribution which managers make in meetings tells us a great deal about effective decision making. Some management teams recognize they need help, and call in consultants to analyse the content and contribution of meetings. Initial observations are discussed, and action taken to ensure that decisions are reached in an optimum manner.

Consultants and trainers tend to concentrate on using fairly simple models which reflect the level of social interaction. The work of Rackham, Carlisle, Pedlar and others is used to analyse contributions.

Most researchers and practitioners in social interaction use the original research of Bales to examine how groups reach decisions. This involves examining the sorts of contributions that managers make in meetings. This could be quite simple, and entail examining who talks to whom. In this case, the researcher would want to isolate the dominant members in the group and examine the social interaction that exists between them.

They can do this simply by logging the meeting, timing the comments from members and devising an intricate network, called a sociogram, which highlights the frequency and direction of communication (see Fig. 9.1).

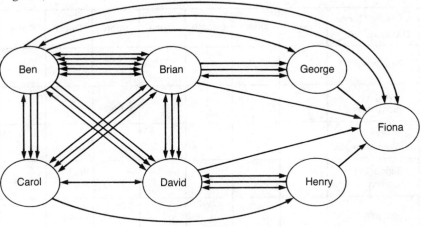

Key:

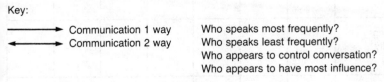

Communication 1 way   Who speaks most frequently?
Communication 2 way   Who speaks least frequently?
                             Who appears to control conversation?
                             Who appears to have most influence?

Fig. 9.1 Sociogram of a departmental meeting

The sociogram outlines the contributions, to whom they are directed, and from where they come. This helps managers analyse the dominant members of the group and work on developing relationships with those with whom they do not normally communicate. The rationale is that groups of managers generally make 'better quality' decisions when a group facilitator or trainer can help the group identify factors which hinder them in making quality decisions.

Behaviour analysis

After watching a meeting start and the contributions develop from different managers, it is possible to assess the direction the meeting is taking. It is possible to identify whether the meeting is orientated in a positive fashion towards achieving a decision or course of action, or whether it is floundering and achieving very little.

An observer, even without much experience, can make use of the *Meeting Assessment Sheet* (MAS) which helps identify the different behavioural styles that are being brought into play (see Fig. 9.2). It is possible to use the MAS to answer the following questions:

Category \ Name	Ben	Brian	George	Fiona	Henry	David	Carol
Proposing							
Giving information							
Seeking information							
Supporting building							
Disagreeing							
Defending/ attacking							
Blocking/ difficulty stating							
Testing for understanding							
Summarizing							

Fig. 9.2 Behavioural Analysis Assessment Sheet

- Who talked to whom?
- How often was the communication reflected?
- How often did the comments flow just in one direction?
- Who is spoken to most frequently within the group?
- Who contributes little or is referred to infrequently?
- Can you identify any cliques within the larger group?
- Who made the decisions?
- Did a small clique of managers influence events? How did they do this?

- Who held up the group in reaching decisions?
- What style did different managers use to reach a conclusion?

These issues can be discussed at length after a meeting. It is best if a group facilitator is present, who will be able to feed back the information in a constructive manner.

Behavioural styles

Going one stage further, it is useful to examine the contributions from managers at a meeting. Some may come with a very dry, analytical attitude which destroys any new creative ideas. Others spend too much time on procedure and too little on the task on hand. It is important to note each manager's style and examine how this influences the quality of decisions reached.

Again, a certain amount of data has to be collected. The best method for assessing contributions is to examine the behavioural style which people can display and then relate these styles to a scoring system (see Fig. 9.2).

Consider carefully the following categories of behaviour and be prepared to analyse *your* behaviour next time you are in a meeting.

Proposing

Behaviour that falls under this category relates to statements which project or put forward a new idea or concept. Examples include, 'I propose we allocate 30 minutes of this meeting to thrashing out the key points', or 'I propose we form a working party which can feed back its conclusions in two weeks'. This approach is positive and forces managers to reconsider their attitude.

Giving information

This is positive behaviour which helps meet the requirements of others. Here the manager freely gives information, facts, data and opinions. Examples include, 'If you let me have a precise idea of your specifications for the new system I will be able to provide you with all the relevant data', or 'Let me tell you about what my department's research has uncovered.'

Seeking information

This is the opposite of the style above. Instead of giving information, this style is concerned with collecting facts, such as 'Tell me about Roy's conclusions and how these will affect the production schedule.'

Supporting building

This behaviour is positive and seeks to create alliances and build bridges between managers. The purpose might be to develop a proposal or extend a proposal made by others: 'I think that John's idea for restructuring the departments is fine, I have similar thoughts. I am sure that if John and I can get together and work out our differences, we could arrive at the right solution'.

Disagreeing

Disagreement by itself is not a bad or poor style. We all need to become slightly more analytical and critical in meetings. This style goes beyond normal criticism. This style reflects the manager who sees nothing good in a new idea and finds ten ways for making it fail, rather than thinking of one positive idea to help it along.

A manager who uses this style all the time wants to get his own way. He has made up his mind and does not want the facts to confuse him! Typical examples include, 'There is no way that new budget will be accepted by my team,' or 'It is ludicrous, we have never needed to look at an incentive scheme for my department'.

Defending/attacking

Attack is one stage beyond disagreeing. Instead of being negative about an idea, this approach can actually be used to attack a person or a position. It can be very personal and is not a very good method for reaching agreement. It offers little by way of constructive criticism. Defending behaviour is concerned with protecting your own position at any cost.

Statements which reflect the *attacking* approach include, 'George, is this another one of your hare-brained ideas? I would have thought that since the incident last year, you would have learned your lesson'.

Defending statements include, 'You know my position on temporary staff, I will not allow them in my Department. I don't care what you do,

I'll fight you all the way up to the chairman'.

These styles help win the battle, but not the war. They are useful as delaying tactics, but if managers use them too often, they find they soon lose support at meetings.

Blocking

This is similar to the style above, but blocks a proposal. It could be used as a delaying tactic because the statements don't include a rationale for what was said. This approach blocks a proposal or states a problem but does not *propose a remedy*. Examples include, 'There is no way they will stand for that,' or 'Take it from me, it'll never work. We tried this sort of thing before and it was disastrous. Take my word for it, do it the way we have always done it'.

Testing for understanding

This is a much more positive manoeuvre. The speaker seeks to establish whether others attending the meeting have fully understood what has been said. This is very much a 'gatekeeper's role' ensuring that all understand the limitations or the benefits of an approach.

Statements include, 'Tell me George, did you say you would provide resources for the new research assistant, and if so, what are the implications for others at this table,' or 'Could you take the committee through paragraph 3a again please? I think a number of us found difficulty taking it all in'.

Summarizing

This behaviour is positive and aims to restate the progress that the meeting has made so far. 'Well, Henry, we have heard your idea for reducing advertising expenditure, and we have heard Frank's idea for employing other PR agents. What action can we take to get the best value for money?'

It is clear that in many statements, managers portray a variety of styles and behaviours. For instance, the manager adopting a *proposing* style may also reflect *supporting/building* and *summarizing* in his contributions. Managers reflecting the *disagreeing style* may also exhibit elements of *defending/attacking*.

Knowing when managers are using specific styles is very helpful. Once you have detected a manager, for instance, being extremely negative about a new proposal, instead of attacking you should aim to draw him out and examine his data, and his prejudices. 'Tell me Sam, you do not appear to have a lot of confidence in the new project. You said it did not work when they implemented it in your last company. To help us reach a decision, could you take us through your major objections, and elaborate in some detail on your past experiences.'

If the answer to this is 'negative' or clearly 'inadequate' then you must respond. 'Sam, I was disappointed that we couldn't share some of your thoughts, because it would have helped us evaluate the proposal, but since the negative aspects of the project do not appear major, can we now progress in a positive manner, and consider the ways by which this project can help us improve our competitive edge.'

This analytical approach is very useful and will help you and your team of managers to create more effective meetings. There are only nine styles demonstrated here; there are many more, but these are the most obvious. Take twenty minutes out of your next meeting to assess the styles which different managers use. Use the Behaviour Analysis Assessment Sheet (BAAS) (see Fig. 9.2) to help you.

Putting your analysis to good use

Taking notes and working with the BAAS for ten to twenty minutes will improve your skill in identifying specific behaviours and will also help you in counteracting the negative, delaying tactics which characterize too many meetings. You will also learn a great deal about *your own* behaviour.

For instance, which is your most dominant style? If you use one style to the detriment of others, you may be not maximizing your potential both in meetings and in communication generally. I have observed a manager who evaluated everything that was said! He never gave speakers a chance to expand on a good idea. He was always looking for ways to make it fail, analysing every element. A good idea would never ever be presented and successfully pass his glance.

Other managers may do the opposite, and spend too much time creating new, innovative ideas, but never use their critical faculties to ensure that their proposals really could be brought to life.

It is clear that there is no one best style. There are a variety of styles which should be used in different circumstances. For example, do you spend too much time *seeking information*? What happened the last time you adopted the *summarizing* style? Did you find your attempts to clarify the issues and viewpoints helped the group reach a better quality decision faster? The last time you used the *attacking* style, how did you do? How did you feel? Was it a positive feeling? Did you spend too much time paying back old debts or playing politics?

According to Rackham *et al.* the most frequently used behaviours tend to be *proposing* and *giving information.* We spend too much time volunteering information, probably in support of our own case, but little time *seeking information* and *clarifying* and *summarizing.* We can spend even less time *building bridges,* and too much time being negative, blocking ideas we do not like.

Next time you attend a meeting, try some new behaviours. If you spend a disproportionate amount of time *seeking information,* why not try *summarizing* for a change? Instead of volunteering viewpoints and information, seek clarification from others. Adopt the non-directive questioning technique, and find out the real objections that managers have to new ideas. Instead of evaluating what people say, rephrase their response and feed it back to them. This should give you a better understanding of their position.

For example, your boss says to you, 'I am unhappy with the way your department dealt with the last project.' You should restate the emotion and feedback, 'So you are unhappy about our last project.' He then says, 'Yes, I don't believe it was handled diplomatically.' You say, 'Diplomatically?' And so the conversation continues. Using the reflective, non-directive technique, you are able to find out a great deal more about the problem, rather than just relying on being *told.* This style has helped many management teams improve their effectiveness.

This style of looking at contributions really does pay dividends and is a very useful learning *vehicle.* Learning how decisions are influenced, and how *crazy* decisions are agreed, forces many managers to examine their style and that of their colleagues.

When the requisite level of trust exists, it may be appropriate to introduce others to the idea of examining group contributions. Given the right environment, where managers are free to reflect on their thoughts and feelings regarding the contributions which they make, it is possible to build a strong and cohesive team of individuals who are committed to developing their level of inter-personal decision making.

Effective management of meetings

This chapter has focused upon a number of problems central to effective meetings management. In many organizations, meetings can be the greatest source of time wasting. This can be especially true in the public sector. Adopting a new approach to managing meetings can have payoffs for all. Bear in mind the following points and you, too, should be able to get more out of meetings.

- Pay attention to the way meetings are organized. The structure by which meetings are held is less important than the issues under discussion. Ensure that there is some balance between constitution and procedure, and the nature and content of the items on the agenda.
- Ensure that the chairman is skilled and trained in his art. Do not put all the responsibility for directing the meeting on him. *You* have a responsibility for making meetings work. If the chairman is unskilled or not assertive, do something about it. Don't just complain afterwards.
- Remember the 80/20 rule. Ensure that more than 20 per cent of those attending have a positive comment to make, otherwise you'll not be optimizing the potential and experience of those present. Try to adopt a flexible style and 'carefully' introduce others in to the debate, to ensure that all views have been heard and considered.
- Fear of looking foolish can stop many managers contributing. Try to generate the type of meeting that encourages new ideas.
- Avoid politics. Although it is endemic within any organization, try to minimize its effects and deal with agenda items in a logical way.
- Design agendas with speed and efficiency in mind. Why deal with volumes of items in a poor way, when you can deal with the high priority items in a professional manner? Don't make agendas too long.
- Prioritize items on the agenda.
- Reject 'Any other business'.
- Introduce time limits and avoid Parkinson's Law.
- Don't confuse *attendance* with *performance*
- Use 'one liners' for speedy and accurate minutes.
- Use the pre-meetings planner (PMP). Use it as a business aid to find out the information you need about the *really* important items on the agenda. Don't use it too often, or it will fail and fall into disrepute.
- Be aware that when you delegate work, or a specific task, to a sub-

committee or working party, you are clear about what you expect them to achieve. If you give out a general brief, without guidance or parameters, don't expect too much in return! Think clearly about issues before delegating them to a committee. Remember, ten hours of chaos can be avoided with one hour of planning.

- Pay attention to the process in meetings. Assess the major contributors and try to identify their style of contribution.
- Ensure that you try alternative styles in meetings and try to adopt a *win* attitude.

Chapter 10

Solving the paperwork problem

Paperwork is probably one of our biggest time wasters. Imagine you arrive at the office, ready for the demands of the day. What is the first thing that greets you? Paperwork. It leaps from the desk and occupies your time and your talents for too long. You say to yourself, 'When I've got rid of this paperwork I'll really be able to get on with something important'. Depending on where you work, paperwork can either be a minor annoyance, or a major barrier to your effectiveness.

Many managers suggest that as they move up the promotion hierarchy, they move away from their technical specialism and develop more of an overseeing role. In other words they become real managers. They develop many and varied responsibilities and, at the same time, have to extend their expertise, understanding and skills, to do a good job. They have to look at problems from different angles and negotiate with other managers and technical experts in addition to attending progress meetings, etc. In other words, they have to co-ordinate work in order to 'make things happen'.

Of course, the trouble with this is that eventually you find more and more paperwork arriving on your desk. You have somehow to read, collate, understand, co-ordinate and store the paperwork. If you are a natural bureaucrat perhaps you will find this a delight, but I assume you bought this book to improve your effectiveness. So read on. Let's look at the paperwork jungle.

Paperwork: where does it come from?

Someone, somewhere is preparing information for your consumption. He is probably not aware of your needs, so he feels that lots of information will be of value to you.

You, on the other hand are experiencing a paperwork overload and haven't the time to consume the paper. If only you could digest the information you need. If you have 'general responsibility' for a project you will receive all the documentation, whether you need or want it. If you are unlucky, you will probably receive two or three copies of material from different sources. Just to confuse, you will receive several updated copies of the same material, but you are too busy to sort through the piles of information on your desk. You'll probably end up going to a meeting with the wrong information.

Unfortunately, as managers rise through the organizational hierarchy, their name is added to countless circulation lists. Also, those who draw up these circulation lists frequently neglect to update them.

Clearly, the accumulation of paper is one big problem, but another one is even more serious. How do you *deal* with paperwork?

Many managers deal with the paperwork as it arrives on the desk. This is a grave mistake. I have frequently seen colleagues wading through mountains of trivial paperwork and never really dealing with the important information until it is too late, or they are too tired and past their best for the day to do a good job.

Another major mistake is to deal with the 'easy stuff' first, i.e. respond to memos, letters, etc. Surely this could be delegated to the right level. Many managers take a delight in composing letters that would shine in literary circles, but unfortunately they are not being effective managers; they are fulfilling some need to be regarded as 'men of letters'.

Many find it difficult to use the resources at their disposal. They fail to recognize that their secretary or personal assistant or the girl in the typing pool is there to provide a service for them. They commit the cardinal sin. *They're not managing, but doing the jobs of others.* Of course, there are circumstances when the manager has to take the lead and do important paperwork, but this should not create a precedent for dealing with trivial matters. The key to managing paperwork is developing a sense of balance.

Regarding balance, many find it hard to develop different techniques and approaches to different kinds of work. Throughout our lives, we develop expertise and discover techniques which help us do our work.

A common mistake is to apply a method or technique that works in one case to every situation. This is where balance is important. Managers must always be open to *working smarter not harder.* They must constantly be looking for strategies and techniques that will help them do a better job, more effectively. This applies especially to paperwork. Let's move on and look at some sensible advice which has helped managers combat the paperwork jungle!

What can you do?

First, you must clarify your objectives. You should be concerned with dealing with the 'bumf' more speedily and more effectively. Saving time through paperwork management releases time for you to do what managers are paid to do, i.e. solving difficult problems and making 'things happen'.

Can you envisage a time when your staying late at the office and taking paperwork home can be justified by special circumstances? If you are not willing to make this commitment *now*, you haven't really accepted that first you have a paperwork problem, and secondly that you want to solve it!

Part of this process involves exploring the nature of your work and deciding on criteria for dealing speedily with your paperwork. This is all part of your 'action plan'. It starts now.

Keep a log as recommended in Chapter 2. See how much of your time is devoted to paperwork. Can you measure, quantify or justify the value of it?

What type of work is it?

Ask yourself these questions:

- Where does the paperwork come from?
- Which department inundates you with information?
- Is the material for action or information?
- Could you survive without the information?
- What would be the consequences for others with whom you work?

Paperwork itself is of little value: only the information it contains is valuable. Ask yourself, is the information that I need to do a good job available? Do I get it? If not, why not? A large number of people can spend their time providing information in some form or other. They believe the information is valuable, accurate and meets your needs. Have you ever spent time speaking to these people and explained your real needs?

Can you identify the person from whom the paperwork flows? You have probably picked the boss! Are you the subject of over delegation?

This is a difficult problem. Do you confront your boss and risk the 'slings and arrows', or do you just hope it will stop? Well, so long as you do a good job, it won't stop. In fact, the faster you do the work, the more will appear. You are fulfilling his expectations. He selected the right man for the job. I'm afraid you'll have to learn how to be more assertive and 'manage your boss' (see Chapter 7).

Is a large proportion of your paperwork related to open-ended queries that require a great deal of research and information gathering? If so, one of the biggest problems is trying to get started. Sometimes it appears that the work is so 'insurmountable' that you put off the job till you have more time. Of course it's a vicious circle. You never have more time. If you are not careful you will rush an important job and perhaps make mistakes.

Take action

To be really effective at managing paperwork you would be wise to address yourself to some of the points in the sections which follow below.

If the paperwork is so vast, decide on objectives, detail the information you require, and take some form of action. If you haven't the data, contact someone who has. Make deadlines. Plan ahead and take one step at a time. The alternative is to rush and risk botching a job.

Is the paperwork related to a problem which you should have solved, but haven't? Managers often have the same recurring paperwork because they failed to do the job *right first time*. The 'it will do attitude' is not worthy of the successful manager. So get your act together, and cut out all the future recurring problems which gnaw at your time. *Do it now* and *do it right*.

Training

Does the paperwork create problems for you and others because you don't have the skills and expertise to do a good job? In today's technological world, when change is accelerating at an ever increasing rate, it is hardly surprising to find that managers do occasionally need coaching or training. What is difficult to establish is that they do not always openly communicate their needs. The problem here is that none of us wishes to appear a fool. So we tend not to tell others of our anxieties. If this shielded ignorance permeates the whole organization, it is not so surprising that paperwork takes up so much of everybody's time.

This leads ultimately to a situation where people are ignorant of the need to maintain paperwork flows and procedures. If we are unaware of the need for systems, but continue adhering to them, we are in danger of developing a 'counter-culture', where the *bureaucracy runs counter to the true aims of the company*.

We all know of those who worship 'paperwork and procedures', and we must guard against outmoded paperwork systems prevailing, and seek new ways of managing. Through training, we can avoid the badge of 'bureaucrat'.

Delegated *up*!

Are you the focus of work which is delegated *upwards* from your subordinates? Don't laugh. Managers quite often realize this only after analysing their paperwork problems. Many are afraid to admit that this happens. They fear someone will find out that they have hired unsuitable subordinates or else they are afraid to tell their staff to take some responsibility or pull their socks up. Poor management practice prevents the problem being solved. The good manager solves problems by facing up to them and by training his staff to accept responsibility, for whatever may be his problems, he has to live with the consequences.

Deciding on priorities

Decide now on your priorities. Which paperwork merits your attention? Should you direct yourself to analysing reports which form the basis for an essential meeting, or spend your time collating important market research information? Clearly, the decision is yours. If you value your time you will not spend it writing routine memos or responding to trivial paperwork.

What then are the *key priorities*? How are you judged? What criteria are used to differentiate between you and your staff? Bear these in mind. *Are you spending your time the best way that you can, right now?*

What are your paperwork priorities? List them, then attach relative values, i.e. 'A' being most important, 'B' being quite important, and so on. Looking at your work in this way should help you to 'realize your contribution'. This will also help you to delegate and train others to take the routine, steady-state work from you, to leave you to spend your time planning and managing for the future.

If you have difficulty estimating your 'A' priority work, ask yourself, 'What has maximum payoff for the organization?'

Now that you have decided on your priorities, make plans to work and complete a 'measurable' and 'valuable' aspect of the 'A' work every day. If you achieve the high priority, the low priority work will look after itself.

A sense of balance

Don't try to do all 'A' work every day. It's too demanding. Introduce some balance with other work being included to increase variety.

Do it now!

Do the 'A' work now, early in the day. Don't do the routine work first and promise the harder work afterwards. You will have wasted the best part of the day on trivial chores.

Now that you plan to be 'super-effective', ask yourself what strategies and skills you will need to develop, to do it *right first time*. Compile a list. You will probably find that you will identify skills which relate to inputting and outputting information, in other words reading and writing. Chapter 11 deals with the skills of speed reading and writing for results and has been specifically designed to help you make the most of your time.

To be really effective at managing paperwork you should address yourself to some of the following points.

Train others to be selective

If your secretaries or assistants do not deal with the paper problem it may be because of the training you have or have not given them. They are not mind readers. You probably don't realize it, but you are wasting one of the most precious resources of all, people. Once you have realized this great truth, you can move on.

Once you realize your assistants can help you, they can act as filters, dealing with certain work themselves and letting the really serious stuff go through to you. But they can only do this if you train them well. You can start by explaining and communicating your 'priorities'. This can be done by developing a flagging system, i.e. any paperwork which arrives at their desks, from you, should have clear instructions regarding the desirable actions to be taken. In addition, you can indicate importance by a colour code or some other system.

Training must be complete; you have to ensure that all your staff know what you mean. If you are really successful your coding system might become a regular feature in your department.

So, now they know what you want. But are they aware of what you do? Spend time with your staff, explain the main duties you perform. This should be obvious, but many subordinates are unaware of what their bosses really do.

When they know what you do, why not tell them about your targets and key result areas? Once they understand the rationale behind your actions, they become clearer on the criteria you adopt to deal with particular work.

Why write a letter when you can use the phone?

Managers often can spend a great deal of their time composing complicated letters. Would it not be wise to use the phone instead? (Or if circumstances permit, delegate the work to the *right level*.)

If you choose to use the phone, ensure that the basic details of the conversation are recorded somewhere. Yes, it might mean you have to write a letter, but your objectives will be clearer, and you can begin '. . . to confirm our telephone call . . .' etc. and then go on to specify, in short, precise terms, the conditions and content of any agreement made on the phone.

Much time is wasted 'drafting' letters, memos and reports. It takes time for some people to admit to this problem, but once they have, they are halfway to creating their own solution.

One final point. When using the phone be judicious. Don't let telephone conversations get out of hand and become a big *time waster*.

Take *some* form of action

Whatever happens, take some action. When you pick that paper out of the in-tray, promise to do something with it! I don't mean you have to deal with the problem completely there and then, but what you can do is take *some* form of action, no matter how small.

Avoid the pending tray

You must not, however, glance at the paper, decide not to make a decision, and place it in *pending*. This is disastrous. One day you will be confronted with all this paperwork which needs some action! Urgent or complex work will tend to build up in the overfull pending tray.

Memory is not enough

'Difficult' or 'open-ended work' tends to fill up the trays. The reason is that the work might be very complicated or time-consuming. You make a mental note and forget the action needed to be taken. The next time you sift through the tray, you are surprised that so much important work has been neglected. You haven't been selective. Your memory is not sufficient to control the urgent demands on your time. You have to become more disciplined and develop a systematic approach. For goodness sake use the daily planning diary.

Take some action, no matter how small. Decide on your objectives. Examine the information you need to collect or to facilitate an answer. Set targets, request information by a set date. Ask your assistant to keep you posted at set times and, finally, set a date, once a week before you need to respond, to ensure you have done it *right first time*.

Review reports

Does a great deal of information arrive on your desk that is not relevant, but noted for your information? If so request your assistant, secretary, etc., to filter out the irrelevancies.

If you receive lots of reports and find them too voluminous to cope with, ask your assistants to prepare a one-page report outlining the major features. They could also detail the advantages and disadvantages of actions to be taken, and assess the consequences for you and your department.

Although initially this might make you unpopular, you will be helping them to develop and get an appreciation of the type of work to which they aspire. Perhaps when they reach your level, they will remember this valuable experience and thank you.

Review mailing lists

Ask your secretary to review or update the mailing lists she develops, and the mailing lists which feature your name. It should be obvious that you have to filter or cut down the trivia, and address yourself to the really important work.

Summary

How did you do? Did you find that you are victim of the 'paperwork jungle'? If so here are a few reminders, a checklist, to help you manage better:

- Recognize, first, that paperwork is time-consuming and that it can and does eat into your time.
- Be prepared and committed to reducing it.
- Deal with paperwork properly. Decide on the order in which you are going to tackle it.
- Use the resources at your disposal, i.e. your staff. They are trained to make life easier for you, so you can make the *big* decisions.
- Clarify your objectives.
- Decide now on criteria for dealing with a full tray of paperwork.
- Examine where the work comes from.
- Discover who generates all this information and why.
- Beware of work that is 'delegated up' from your subordinates.
- Decide on priorities.
- Develop a sense of balance. Vary the intensity of the work upon which you are working.
- Train others to be selective.
- Don't write a letter when you can use the phone.

Chapter 11

Saving time through writing and reading

A great deal of time can be wasted either reading managerial 'information' or writing replies to memos, reports and letters. If you have kept your time log up to date, you will realize just how much time you spend doing these things.

Some time ago, I worked with a large company in the telecommunications industry. When the managers examined how much time they spent reading and writing, they were amazed. Although some had always been aware that it took up time, they did not realize just how much. When we related the time log to Minzberg's research into 'what managers do', they were shocked that their 'reading and writing' activity took up so much time and really was a key result area.

The extent to which the information possessed by senior managers was accurately transmitted to others reflected the effectiveness of those managers. After recognizing that they spent so much time doing these things, we decided to take action in order to maximize their available time.

Writing for results

How often have you started to write a draft letter or memo and then found that after your efforts you still have not expressed yourself as clearly as you wished? You may find that you have written much, but said little, or that there is a great deal of ambiguity in your writing. How do you become a better writer?

Let us get back to absolute basics. You will require a reasonable grounding in grammatical English, but do not be put off from writing because you have failed to understand all the rules of grammar! You do not have to be a literary genius.

Write to express, not impress

This is the main problem faced by many managers in this area. They confuse *expression* with *impression*. Instead of stating their case, they write to the audience. They write to impress their peers, or, even worse, their boss. Why do they spend time like this? Because they believe that 'massaging their image' will gain them promotion, or put them in a more favourable position within the hierarchy.

Where do we start?

We must first recognize that very few people write well, and that our training in school, college and university, which may have suited us for an academic paper or thesis, will probably not provide us with the rigour, straight talking, and brevity required by industry and commerce.

Reference to memos tells us that many are too verbose and too long, whereas they could project the same message using fewer words and avoid confusing the reader!

How can we learn to write and communicate our thoughts clearly?

People who write a great deal master this skill quickly. Journalists are a case in point. Look at most newspaper articles and you will find that journalists communicate concisely with ease. Whichever newspaper we consult, we generally find a high standard of clear communication. As we move from the simple message in the daily tabloids to the more serious press, we find differences which relate to expression and detail, as well as to depth of investigation. The major point is that newspapers are an efficient form of communicating world events speedily. If you require a thorough analysis, you will have to purchase a more serious paper which meets your needs. If you only require an overview, you may decide to choose from the 'tabloids'.

What we as managers are looking for is a style which conveys a message concisely. We do not always have to write memos as if they were to appear in the *Telegraph*, *Guardian* or *Financial Times*!

Gunning, an expert in writing style, suggests that managers should develop a much clearer, more effective writing style if they wish to express their thoughts with clarity. In Gunning's book, *The Technique of Clear Writing*, he develops what he calls his *fog* index, which is a complex equation listing and quantifying the acceptability of reading material to a specific audience. It is not necessary here to go into detail, but factors which are considered are the length of sentences, the number of sentences with polysyllabic words, the average number of syllables in words, etc.

This is the method by which we can establish the degree of difficulty associated with a set text. A random sample of the text can be chosen and the average number of words counted for each sentence. You may wish to isolate and record the number of words in the text with more than three syllables and so on. Using Gunning's formula, it is possible to assess the 'reading age' of the target population. The reading age relates to the number of years of formal education the audience has received.

By comparing the difficulty of the text with the ability of the reader it is possible to establish the degree to which individuals will have ease or difficulty in reading and understanding. Reading is easy, understanding takes analysis. For example, the tabloids require a very low reading age. Most children of eight and above should have no difficulty in understanding the writing. The better quality newspapers require the reader to have a better command of formal English and some expertise or knowledge of the subject-matter.

The major point to make here is that journalists and newspapers decide on their target market and write precisely for it. Unfortunately, this is not always true in management circles. Many managers do not consider their readers; instead they spend too much time trying to impress them with their expertise and flair!

Many write at a *fog* index that is way above the audience's ability. Sentences are too long, conveying too many ideas at once, and the words which comprise the sentence are multi-syllabic. To avoid 'turning people off' from reading what we have written, we can follow a few short rules, which should do a great deal to clarify our intentions and objectives, reflect the spirit in which the memo or letter is written, and improve the reader's comprehension.

Sentence length

Sentences should be kept short. We should avoid long convoluted sentences peppered with commas, semicolons and the like. The words which comprise the sentence should be simple, not complex. If the reader has to think through the 'meaning' of words then the message will be distorted or not received!

Use familiar terms

Familiar terms and phrases should be used where possible. If we use complex terms which complicate the issues, then the effectiveness of the message must be in question.

Avoid passive verbs

Verbs must be active, and we should try to avoid using those that are passive and do not illustrate our point to the intention of the letter. To go one stage further, some writers suggest that it often helps if we write as we talk. However, this should be viewed with some caution, as we should never degenerate into using phrases which mean little to others.

Introduce illustrative terms

When we write, we draw a picture for our readers. Those who cannot express and communicate their message in colourful and illustrative terms will not have attracted the reader to the material. If the reader feels that the information is boring and poorly expressed, it is likely that the 'message' will never be fully received, understood and appreciated by those who are expected to read and benefit from it.

Relate to the experience of the audience

If you are aware of your audience, it may be necessary to relate to the experience of your readership, but be aware that you can make too many assumptions and miss or disguise your message in jargon.

Creativity and flexibility

In writing, it is important to develop flexibility of style and a degree of creativity. Clearly, what is sufficient for a memo to your staff may be grossly inadequate for an important customer or your boss. Knowing to whom you write and why should help you to adopt a flexible and creative approach.

Reports

Reports are the curse of all managers! Reports *should* be able to provide information upon which others make decisions and take action. What we should aim to do is to write the report in a logical manner, and concentrate on the conclusions and recommendations. Managers are not too interested in the methodology or the way you did the report. They like to flash straight through to the conclusions and recommendations.

Some managers spend too much time analysing the problem and stating how difficult it will be to take decisive action. Instead of stressing the negatives, we should orientate ourselves to one-line statements that are positive in nature, and express precisely how we can take the necessary action. Let us look for the one way of making something succeed rather than ten ways to make it fail!

The recommendations should state clearly, in a step-by-step approach, the 'how' or the approach the company can adopt to ensure that the *right action is taken at the right time*!

We should avoid 'woolly' phrases and try to guide the reader through our recommendations. If you are writing the report and you really do want the main body of the report to be accepted, you must ask yourselves a question, before you finally complete your draft:

'In how many ways can this fail?'

Answering this question should focus your attention upon criteria which are going to be in the minds of those who will read your report. You should always append a summary page outlining precisely the content of the recommendations.

Reading for results

Let's look at the same problem from a different angle. Instead of your being the writer let us assume that you are the reader!

How many of us have really learned to read *properly*? We may be able to read in the literal sense but can we read for results? Ask yourself, why do I read?

There are a number of reasons. Here is the first consideration: the purpose for which we read determines the approach we should adopt when reading.

Reading to disseminate information

We read to find and disseminate information. This might involve consulting information that may be of value, not now, but in the future.

If the reason for reading information is related to high priority work, we will adopt a different style from reading material that may be read only for interest.

Reading for action

This consists of reading reports and assessing the worth of the information contained therein, in order to take some action or make a decision.

Reading to learn

When we learn to read, we are spending time pursuing an activity which helps us develop new skills, behaviours, knowledge, etc.

Whatever the purpose for reading, we must develop flexibility to tackle the material in different ways. Clearly, reading for *action* requires a critical style that may be not required. If we are reading for low priority *information*.

Reading techniques

When reading, do we have to understand the details of every paragraph and every sentence? Not necessarily so; it depends on our purpose. If we are reading for *information*, such a style will not be appropriate, but if we are reading to *learn* a new technique, it may be important. Reading for learning will require a more studious approach, but, again, it is not necessary to adhere to every word of the text.

The difficulty of the text will also determine our reading speed in terms of whether we read intently, rapidly or skim. Reading intently, or reading word by word or phrase by phrase is appropriate for text which is difficult but also essential to our needs. It is pointless, however, to plough through detailed specifications if the content is of little value to our work.

Do not read books, *use* them!

Often you can observe managers reading detailed information that they do not require now or in the future. They are breaking the most important rule of all: books are not meant to be read, but to be used! If you are reading for pleasure, then the joy of the words and the literature are important to the value you place on the reading experience, but why adopt this approach for *work*?

How to improve your reading technique

Here are some general rules which may help you to increase the speed of your reading and enable you to get through all the information which arrives in your in-tray.

'Gears'

When going uphill in a car we tend to be careful about the gears we use. The more difficult the hill, the lower the gear. Why don't we adopt the same approach when reading? There are a number of ways we can tackle a report. We can skim the content and highlight the most important part, and then return to the beginning of the text. Do we start here? Why should we? We can start wherever we wish.

When we hit the first difficult part of the text, what do we do? We change down and start reading, 'sentence by sentence' or 'word group to word group'. If the material becomes gradually more difficult, we have to slow right down to reading word by word. After we leave the difficult section we forget to change gear. This is a problem from which many suffer. They fail to recognize that they are over the difficult terrain and that they should be speeding up their consumption of words per minute.

A normal reading speed is 300 w.p.m. When we slow right down, we can take in words very slowly, think about their context, meaning and structure, and then regress back into the material. In fact, we may regress on a number of occasions but this tactic will give us understanding. Skimming will not. You will note that you often have to force yourself to speed up after you have finished reading the difficult parts of a report. Think how much time you can waste by forgetting to change gear through the less important material.

Gaining general understanding

If your purpose is to gain a general understanding of the material, there is no need to adopt the word-by-word approach. It is wasteful. The best way to make the most of your time and increase your speed is to take the text line by line and focus only upon phrases. You must not regress; it is a bad habit that many practise. In studying, you have no alternative – you have to understand the mechanics of the situation. For general understanding, the rhythm of your reading speed is at risk. You are required to progress through the text at a uniform speed. Remember, there is no compulsion to read the whole text. You may find it appropriate to read the introduction and the conclusions, get a feel for the text or report, and use the index to focus on issues of relevance to you and your job.

What characterizes the effective reader?

Research suggests that there are many differences between good and poor readers. Good or effective readers have a wide eye-span which enables them to take in more than the poor reader who prefers to read word by word. The effective reader develops rhythm in his reading and can change his style to suit the circumstances. The poor reader regresses frequently, while his successful counterpart moves through the text at a constant rate.

There are times when we should regress, but with too many individuals this is their natural response. Only in special circumstances should we regress, usually with a very difficult text that we have to understand completely. Other texts require a constant reading speed. This approach actually increases comprehension, rather than reducing it!

'Inner speech'

Next time you are in a local library look around and watch people using their 'inner speech' or subvocalization. They mouth the words that they are reading in their heads. This can slow the reader down tremendously, and be a source of merriment for colleagues as well! Inner speech will never take over if you scan or speed read; it only happens when you read word by word! So beware!

Comprehension

Comprehension can also be improved by adopting a much more critical approach.

- Be aware of why you are reading. Ask yourself: 'Why am I reading this material? What will this material help me achieve? Do I need to read it all? Am I reading material which others could read then prepare a short report or precis for me?'

- 'What gear should I use and when? What action can I take to ensure that I develop the skills of the effective reader?'
- When you are reading, ask yourself: 'What does the information tell me? What information would supply my needs? Will this information make my job any easier?
- What authority does the author possess? Is the information reliable, up to date, accurate and relevant?
- How is the information projected to the reader? Is it objective or is there an element of bias? Why?
- Does the author use *reason* or *emotion* in his arguments and statements?
- What is his hidden agenda? What is he trying to say? Has the information influenced your actions and behaviour?
- Assess the information. Has the text author presented his case well or failed? Why has he passed or failed? What criteria have you used to evaluate his efforts? Have you been truly objective?

Finally, there is no one best way to improve your capacity to read and comprehend more, but research suggests that readers can significantly influence their capacity to read through text and improve their comprehension by imitating good readers and developing the discipline to widen the eye span, reduce inner speech, scan and develop rhythm as you move through the text. It is possible to double or treble your speed without sacrificing comprehension. This increase in comprehension should have some impact on your managerial performance and release you for other high priority work.

Likewise, a dedication to *expressing* yourself in written communication should release you to achieve your results!

Chapter 12

Mastering the telephone

You may be unaware that your telephone can be a big time waster. How much time do you spend talking on the phone? Perhaps you do not know precisely, but you will be aware that, sometimes, the technology has made a slave of you. How often do we have to return calls to other managers, customers and suppliers, and find that they are not available? This can develop into a situation where both you and your contact are spending precious time phoning each other without actually getting through.

For calls that are not prearranged, the likelihood of contacting the person you wish to talk to is low. Again the 80/20 rule comes into play. You may find that of the time you spend on the phone only 20 per cent is effective.

A personnel manager from a distillery once told me, 'I just don't know where the work comes from. Every day I pick up the phone I seem to get more and more work.' She was referring to the receiving of calls as opposed to making outgoing calls. Her problem was that she would answer the phone and be as helpful as possible to the person on the other end. Even though an enquiry might come from outside her responsibility, and was the responsibility of her superior, she would try to provide the interested party on the other end of the line with the information needed. It became an obsession to please others.

What happened? Over the years she gained a tremendous reputation for being helpful, not just to her own department, but to every department in the plant. You may see nothing wrong with this, and some may actually applaud her behaviour, but I did not. As with all things in time management, she had not adopted a balanced approach. She had let her friendliness and lack of assertion rule her working day. She was spending all her time helping others achieve their goals, at the expense of her own! She had difficulty achieving results in her key result areas. Her superior wondered what was wrong as she had always been a good worker.

It was only after keeping a time log for three weeks that she realized she spent a tremendous amount of time on the phone. We might expect someone from telephone sales or customer relations to spend as much time on the phone, but the difference was that she was *responding* to, not activating, the communication.

She was an efficient phone user and never wasted unnecessary time, but she was doing the work of others. She did not have sufficient assertiveness to say 'no'!

Once she recognized her problem, she took corrective action to ensure it did not happen again. She learnt new ways of responding, kept notes by her phone to remind her whether the scope of the enquiry really did fit in with her key result areas. She did not become aggressive. She did, however, become a more effective manager by managing the telephone and by becoming more assertive.

Where does your time go?

The time log that we described in Chapter 2 will show how much time you spend on the phone. You can also keep a notepad by the phone with four columns. Each column should be subdivided in the same manner as the telephone log in Fig. 12.1.

TELEPHONE LOG

DATE...

TIME	CALLER	SUBJECT	ACTION

Fig. 12.1 Telephone log

Although it may appear difficult to develop the *discipline* to record the use of the phone, after a week of accurate logging you will be amazed at how much time you can save. The process of keeping a log will act as a prompt, and discipline you to reduce the non-productive element of your telephone conversations.

Time wasters

Incoming calls

If you are constantly on the defensive and have to react rather than activate the phone call, you run the risk of taking on more work than you should. A casual conversation can soon turn into a situation where you end up taking on the work of others. If the call is not related to your area of responsibility – pass it on!

Do you find that you regularly take calls for others who are absent and, by default, end up doing their work? Here the problems lie with your colleagues. You have to be more assertive and have them formally agree to the transfer of calls.

Poor correspondence creates telephone overload

Do you get a large number of phone calls from others because your internal communication, i.e. memos and letters, is inadequate? This can be a major problem. Many staff clearly do not possess the necessary skills or are perhaps too lazy to construct a memo or letter which conveys the required intent and communication. Ask yourself who is responsible for all the calls you receive. You may be responsible! Many phone calls are made in order to correct misconceptions, or to ensure that information presented on paper can be questioned and explained in order to be fully understood. This implies that some ambiguity exists, and the phone call verifies this when questions are asked to establish the degree to which the message has been transmitted accurately.

Reducing wasted time

Analyse the objective of the call

When responding to a phone call, be courteous, but try to find out quickly the *objective* of the call. Do not let the enquiry drag on. Try to structure the conversation so that you can assess the amount of time needed to deal with the enquiry. Then, tell the caller how much time you will be able to spend and the action you will be able to take. If you feel that you are having work passed to you, that is not within your realm of expertise, think again and be assertive. Say 'no'. Try to make alternative arrangements whereby your caller can gain the information required and *you* can continue with your work.

Knowing the appropriate response is a matter of balance. This balance can be seen if the key result areas are clearly and precisely defined. Within the key results, one will be able to examine the degree of overlap of various peoples' work, and the *desirable* level of integration and co-operation between people. Colleagues may rely too much on your expertise and experience, and spend too much time on the phone asking you questions, whereas if *they* were committed to finding out for themselves the full details of the work, they would not be wasting *your* time.

Playing 'tag'

One of the constant problems, which we have all experienced, is playing 'tag' on the phone. You may phone someone several times, probably regarding an important matter, and find that he or she is not available. In return, your contact phones you back, but you are out. And so the process continues. To avoid playing 'tag' you should give clear instructions to your staff, indicating the times when you will be available and waiting for the call, and give clear guidance on the message you wish relayed, so that emergency and high priority calls will always find you at some time of the day.

Outgoing calls

Here, you have much more control of the situation, or so we are led to believe! However, we still find that many managers cannot maintain control. Some do not know when to draw to a close the polite, social conversation. Others jump too quickly from social niceties to 'the business'.

One manager told me of a supplier who always phoned, asked him how the family were keeping and then abruptly turned into the 'sell'. The lack of credibility and genuine concern for 'the family' created the situation in which the manager sought a supplier with better developed 'social skills'.

When making a call do some preparatory work. Before dialling the number, ensure that you have thought clearly about the issues you wish to discuss. Some of the work you talk about will be low priority and routine, but what about the sensitive issues which require a long-term commitment on the part of the person on the other end of the phone?

Cultivate a good telephone manner

It is amazing how many budding careers can be jeopardized by a poor telephone manner. A young manager phoning his senior and discussing issues he does not fully understand is undoing all the good work he has put in over the years.

The hasty comment on the phone, the ill-thought-out response, the speedy reply which tells that you do not fully understand the situation will do no good. You must plan your calls, decide on the issues you wish to discuss, decide on your priorities, the areas where you wish to seek and create agreement, and a closing or summarizing statement which will ensure that both parties have understood the nature, content and outcome of the conversation.

Planning and preparation are the keys to success. Ask any successful salesman and he will tell you the value of the well-mastered and prepared telephone sale. He pursues the technique in a more formal sense, but you as a manager similarly need the technique to influence and persuade others.

One best style

Is there one style which will help you win the day? Certainly not. Many believe that there is one right way, and they never listen to the most important person, the caller on the other end of the phone.

There are too many 'amateur psychologists' who never give any thought to using anything but their 'stereotyped style'. People differ, and if we are talking to others trying to sell ideas, concepts, proposals, etc., it is wise to develop a contingency style, rather than adhere to a rigid routine. The situation, the personalities and the area under discussion all determine the appropriate style and the approach for that occasion. The best style of all is one of *flexibility*, the ability to react, think on your feet, and deal with a variety of personalities and situations.

What can we do?

First, recognize that everybody is different. Different personalities respond differently to the same approach. What will lead to confirmation with one person could lead to an outright rejection with another. Style flexibility is the key.

We make phone calls for a number of reasons. We are usually seeking, confirming, gathering or disseminating information. In concrete terms, we are using the skills of negotiation, persuasion and selling to ensure that our proposals are agreed. What can we do to ensure that not only do we just reduce the time spent on the phone, but also that we actively increase our telephone effectiveness?

Objective setting

Clarify your objectives and know your subject. Do not tell lies! If you are found out, you will never retrieve your credibility! Ensure that you have prepared sufficiently well to establish and meet the objectives you *must* achieve. Before you phone, consider any areas where your colleague or client may need clarification. Be aware of any possible reasons for dismissing your proposals and be prepared to counter them. Above all, prepare, and if in doubt plan again!

Commit your thoughts to paper. For some reason, they will look so much more realistic. You do not have to carry too much information in your head and the well-thought-out notes will appear much more credible over the phone. I do not mean that you should read out your proposals from a card, but have some documentation on paper which will reinforce your arguments, case and proposals, so that if you do fail you know that there was little further action you could have taken to avert failure. In other words, you will know that you did your best.

Standard response

Standard responses are fine so long as those who use them do not read them from a card, or sound as if they are doing so! They sound so wooden and contrived.

Recently, I phoned a DIY superstore to request the prices of some materials. The young man answering the phone said, 'Good morning, thank you for phoning us. My name is David, I hope I can be of assistance. Tell me about your enquiry and I will deal with it as soon as I can.' The voice and obvious reading speed of twenty words per minute told a tale.

The 'standardized response' is excellent in theory, but if the person delivering the response lacks any real enthusiasm and confidence, the message is a disaster. The fact that, following his greeting, I was left hanging on the phone for a further five minutes did not inspire confidence in the store, or in the manager responsible for 'customer relations'.

Improving telephone efficiency

Answerphones

You do not have to run your own business to purchase and use an answerphone. Very few managers always have a secretary available to answer the phone. A close friend gets around this by having an answerphone on his desk. He uses it when he is away or when he is busy working on a key priority. He is no longer simply reacting to others, he is taking the opportunity of regulating his day without alienating his friends and colleagues. He keeps his finger on the pulse.

His message is clear and simple:

'Hello, this is Frank. Sorry I am not available at the moment, but if you leave your name, the time of calling and a short message after the tone, I will get back to you as soon as I can.'

Frank has invested in an answerphone which plays back messages when he phones into the office. He has found that his effectiveness has increased, and he plans to encourage others in his department to follow his example.

Accepting calls

If you can establish a specific hour or so during the day when you can be contacted, those who phone at that time will have their behaviour reinforced, because you will be there to deal with them. If others start using your designated time, you will have to move through the calls quite quickly, in order to complete all your business! This is a built-in motivator to help you get the most out of your telephone time.

Priorities

When you make your outgoing calls, dial them in order of priority. Do not deal with the social phone calls first, leave them till last.

Telephone sales

Telephone selling is a very specialized technique, but a simple understanding of some of the basic principles will help many managers improve their score rate on the phone.

You might not be selling a product, but, on many occasions, you are selling something. Maybe it is an idea to a superior. It may be more than this, perhaps a proposal or an attempt to gather support. It might be simply selling yourself. All these have one thing in common: you have to assess the type of individual you are dealing with, in order to get your own way. If you know the person, you will be aware of his prejudices, his hobby-horses, his objections and his preferences.

What if you do not know him? You have to use the phone to best effect to achieve your goal. You have no idea of the expression on his face when you mention a key word or phrase, you may not even notice his interest in a subject. You have to ensure that you spend sufficient time planning your proposal.

Step one: preparation

Know what you are selling. In other words, write down your objectives for the phone call. As well as establishing rapport, you may wish to develop a longer-term business relationship. You must clarify your objectives. What do you want? Write them down now, otherwise you may find that the recipient of your phone call could guide you into areas which lead you away from your objectives. Listen carefully, and always try to steer it back on course if the conversation has deviated.

Use social conversation to warm up the client or colleague and then to the matter at hand by bridging your social conversation with 'business talk'.

If you are selling an idea or wish to make an appointment for a meeting, use open-ended questions and provide options, e.g. 'Will it be convenient to call on you in your office at Friday at 10 a.m. or Monday at 4 p.m.?' Further to this, you should 'recommend' a time and date, and state the benefits of your preference, e.g. 'The sales projections will be completed on Monday at 12 noon, so we will have the most up-to-date information at our fingertips'.

Addressing objections

Understanding the reasons for refusal is paramount. All good salesmen address the 'objections' of the client. We, as managers, can and should do the same.

Although we might not be selling a product to our colleagues, we are probably in the business of selling ideas. We need the commitment of our colleagues to our goals to make them work. The skills of negotiation are so important to the manager, not just in a formal sense, but, more importantly, in day-to-day transactions.

Transacting business on the phone can create disadvantages for the manager selling an idea or concept. He cannot rely on eye contact or on non-verbal behaviour. He cannot see the facial expression of his colleague. He cannot spot signs of approval or disapproval. In fact, he only has the content of 'what is said and how it is said'. He has no other clues. What can he do, apart from developing his listening skills?

Planning

He has to prepare for the telephone call in the same way as a salesman would prepare for a professional sales call. He has to be aware of the type and variety of questions to ask in order to assess the response. The questions might highlight the *benefits* of the proposal he has to make. The response to the proposal will tell him something about the person on the other end of the line.

All the better for him if the phone call is being made to someone he knows well, otherwise he has to rely on his ability to listen to 'what is being stated, what isn't being stated, and what cannot be stated without help'.

Assess whom you are phoning

Assessing the character or the personality of the recipient of the call, in a number of areas, helps address the typical objections someone may have to a proposal.

Four types of manager

Broadly speaking managers can be split up into four different categories:

- the analytical manager;
- the controlling manager;
- the people manager;
- the creative manager.

They do not fall neatly into these categories all the time. There is some overlap. On some occasions, the style adopted by a particular manager is a combination of the above. Generally, we find that managers tend to portray characteristics of the first and second type, or the third and fourth.

The analytical manager

This is the sort of manager who is a meticulous planner, probably an engineer or accountant who has been trained in following through the precise sequence of events to achieve a given end. This chap likes detail. When you express a new idea to him, he thinks, 'In how many ways can this fail?' He is a critical, analytical type who is keen to inspect ideas, concepts and proposals and apply them to what he knows. He tests them against, the 'state of the art, the way it works now'.

If you can brief yourself on the type of personality this manager possesses, and his 'managerial persona', you will be able to identify his objections, and frame a response which will eradicate them once and for all. You will be carefully enquiring about his views and phrasing your responses accordingly.

The analytical manager is constantly striving for knowledge to improve on the existing system. Although critical, and looking for ways to make things fail, if you can sell your idea in *practical* terms you are on to a winner. If you sell your ideas in a fashion which involves looking outside his current area of expertise or knowledge, you will not succeed.

The analytical manager is not a risk taker. He will expect you to have a fine attention to detail, and your proposals must not disrupt the status quo. If the reality of any proposal or change is significant, you will then have to map out in a clear, short and *pragmatic* way the results you would expect.

Listen to his objections. As soon as you hear the 'analyst' you must focus your attention on tried and trusted methods, on the concrete benefits of your proposals, and the ease of putting them into operation without causing disruption.

Do not, in any circumstances, build visions which require him to have the innovative and creative imagination to see the benefits in the long term. You must stay 'here and now' if you want to influence the analyst.

The controlling manager

In some respects, the controller is similar to the analyst. He is interested in your idea so long as it is practical. He is probably impatient and somewhat authoritarian. He is devoted to bottom line results. Any idea you sell on the phone must be pragmatic, and relate to how he can take 'control' of things. He wishes to control the operation as much as possible. Any suggestion which heightens this 'control, importance, influence and status' is one which will be listened to and implemented.

The controller does not like debate. He wishes to be told, as he would tell others, what, if, when, and how, things will happen. Do not take too long to get your idea across. This manager has results on his mind. Ensure that if the scheme is costly, the payments will be spread out over time to save large resource reallocation. Do not try to be too friendly, this manager is interested only in what the idea can do for him!

The people manager

Selling an idea or proposal to this manager requires an understanding of how it will influence the people, his staff, their security, job satisfaction and their training needs. This manager is friendly and sociable, and will be eager to explore new ideas with you. He has a high need for affiliation, so any proposal must focus upon the positive, rather than the negative, side of change. You may be able to develop a personal relationship with this manager, and this will increase the trust he has in you.

Do not try to force him to make decisions. He has to make up his own mind. He is not interested in power for its own sake, but is a people person and wants to be liked for his innovations. He does not respond well to forced choices or pushy proposals. Your best bet is to plant an idea, let it root and grow and come back later to nurture it!

The creative manager

This manager has much in common with the previous category. He is easily sold on new, creative and innovative ideas. He likes to try a new approach to solving problems. He is enthusiastic and supports a good idea. He is not like the analyst in that he does not like attention to detail. It bores him. You have to sell the idea of the overview.

Do not complicate your call with detail and facts. Ensure that your comments are illustrative and build visions of what could be. He will be highly critical if he feels that your idea is just a rehash of an 'old idea'. If you give him that impression you will have lost for ever.

Clearly, managers do not fall neatly into any of these areas, but you will be able to recognize people and colleagues you work with by reference to some of the traits outlined above. Assessing the type and variety of personality characteristics people possess and the degree to which *you* can establish their typical objections will help you in formulating your ideas. This is particularly important on the telephone, when you have no other cue to a response!

Summary

As telephone and video conferencing become more popular as a means of transferring information, thus reducing travelling time and costs, so the importance of developing your communication, listening and *objection handling skills* will become even more important.

The ability to use the phone well, eradicate the time wasters and actively save time will be very much determined by your ability to think quickly and prepare for all contingencies – *before* you start dialling that number!

Chapter 13

Delegation

Delegation is one of the most discussed, but least practised, of all the managerial skills. Managers who want to make better use of their time can gain premiums by using the delegation process to increase the time available for dealing with key issues, e.g. planning for the future, and thinking about the application of new, innovative methods of management. Most managers recognize that developing this skill frees them for more important work.

Keeping people busy

Managers sometimes confuse delegation with keeping people busy. I have seen instances when managers have given a great deal of work to some staff who are classed as 'lazy'. The reasoning behind it is:

'It is the only way we can keep them working. They are lazy, they have to be directed to do something.'

The real problem here is not the lazy member of staff, but the manager who is using delegation of tasks as an excuse for not doing other things. Clearly there are a number of problems apparent. Motivation of course, but more importantly assertiveness, or rather lack of it, on the manager's side. If the manager genuinely believes that he has to load staff with work to ensure they do work, he must realize and accept that he has a man management problem and do something about it immediately.

Failure to take decisive action could be rooted in inexperience, lack of training or just sheer guts. But what he must do is own up to the problem, take some form of corrective action to ensure it doesn't happen again, and ensure that his behaviour from then on is orientated to 'preventing' this incident arising ever again. Delegation should never be used just to keep people busy!

Managers who delegate well are those who recognize they cannot, and should not, do everything themselves. They understand that a manager's performance is not determined by what he does himself, but how he gets others to achieve (his) targets.

Delegation: achieving results through others

Management is the process of achieving results through others. The manager's key function is to create, build and develop a sound and flexible working team around him. Who will deal with his work when he is away? If on his return, we find that his work is still left undone, what has his team been doing?

The manager's key results are important and must be achieved, whether or not he has been engaged on other projects. If his work only takes place when he is present, it tells us a great deal about his ability to develop teams and lead by example.

We must ask, does he fully utilize the resources around him, or does he think he is indispensable? If he cannot ensure that the high priority work is dealt with even when he is away or involved in other projects, he really must make up his mind to improve his delegation skills.

A good manager is never missed. His team still achieve his results when he is away. Perhaps the team can't dot the i's and cross the t's, but they can take some positive action, no matter how small, to progress work through. If the manager fails to direct them, and give them confidence to do the work, he may spend an increasing amount of his time doing work that he pays others to do!

The poor manager does not have this directive skill and constantly complains that, if only he had a good team around him, he could work wonders. How wrong he is. He has failed to recognize that teams of staff learn by example and training. If the manager has not been sufficiently motivated to provide a good example, or has failed to invest in training his staff, he must suffer the consequences.

Delegation, above all other skills, is that which helps us get more out of the day. We can do this by ensuring that our staff achieve the results we desire, by giving them the authority, confidence, and training to do specific tasks.

But how can we be sure that we can delegate effectively? How can we ensure that we use the abilities and skills of our staff to their best advantage? First, we have to understand that delegation is the key to more effective management, and that using this skill has more payoffs than we may think at first.

Balance and delegation

We delegate for a number of reasons. Getting rid of work is only one of them. As with all time management principles, delegation is a matter of balance. If we delegate too little, we are accused of spending too much time on trivial tasks. If we delegate too much, we may be accused of abdication.

Delegating too little may be a sign that the manager has no real conception of his priorities and key result areas. He may also suffer from a lack of assertion. How easy does he feel about giving work to others? Does he say, 'It's not worth the bother and the hassle, I'll do it myself'? If he does, his staff are managing him. Sooner or later this will affect his effectiveness.

Getting the balance right between delegating too little and too much is difficult, but clearly far preferable to doing everything oneself.

Why delegate?

- Delegation is not just simply a method for giving work to others or keeping them busy, but is a means of allocating work in an optimum manner to those best able and skilled to do it. The guiding principle is, delegate the task as near to the problem as possible and to the person who is most able to fix it.
- Delegation helps managers to differentiate between work which has long- rather than short-term payoffs. Managers should be directing routine, steady-state work as far down the line as possible. In other words, those at the source of the problem are probably best able to deal with it. Managers should be spending more of their time on issues and work that will give long-term payoffs to the company than on short-term trivia.

  Managers who spend too much time on less important tasks are hiding from the real work. They refrain from delegating and claim as an excuse that they are 'too busy'. The effective manager gets rid of the less important work and delegates to the right level. This gives him more time to achieve his key result areas.

- Delegation is a skill which helps managers decide to whom they should direct work. Having a good knowledge of employee strengths and weaknesses helps them to assess who is the most able to complete work. Work is founded upon specialization of labour.

  The manager is paid to achieve results by using the special talents, skills and experience of the people who work with him. He is paid to be selective and use the resources at his disposal for best impact on the 'bottom line'.

- Delegation can be used to develop the experience and skills of junior staff. It is a very useful management development technique. Giving a particular task to a junior manager will help him develop his expertise. This 'coaching' activity will work provided that sufficient guidance is given.
- Delegation is a very useful communication tool. Managers can use delegation as a medium by which their key result areas are communicated to their staff. Knowing what needs to be completed is not enough. Junior managers must experience the 'how', so that they can identify problems when they may take over that task.
- Delegation is a technique which ensures that tasks are completed in the best way, in the shortest time, using the right person.

What are the major barriers to delegation?

As with all time management problems, the barriers are usually self-imposed. All the techniques and workshops in the world will not make an effective delegator out of a poor manager. Commitment, motivation and discipline are essential traits and separate the effective from the ineffective.

We suggest that you ask yourself the question, *'What is the best use of my time right now?'* If the answer to the question is unrelated to the work you are doing, you have a problem. There is only one way to solve it. You must be committed to taking charge, and doing something about the fact that you are doing the *wrong job*!!

Your goals

Are you really aware of your goals and objectives? Many managers go to work each day, adhere to the system, complete the steady-state work and have little idea of any future goals they wish to achieve. Working life, to them, consists of the chore, the routine, feeding the system, looking forward only to the end of the working day, and the knowledge that they will be doing the same chores the next day. They have lost their enthusiasm and their drive. They are stuck. Their attitude will stop any further career advancement.

To break out from the mundane, the trivia, to escape the system, and be more in control of your life and your career, you must set targets which have real meaning, for you and the organization.

Your key task is to move towards these targets, improving your experience and giving your confidence a boost all along the line.

What to do

Writing down your key result areas and identifying tangible, realistic and measurable indicators of your success is a worthwhile exercise, even if you have done it before! If you cannot, with some degree of certainty, explain your purpose in clear concise terms, it is likely that you have lost your direction and focus, and are hiding in the system!

Long-term payoffs

How much of your time do you spend on long-term payoff activities? Probably too little. Many managers claim that the long-term perspective in their company has temporarily been shelved while a rush job is completed. How often does the quick rush job, the firefighting, the running around get in the way of long-term results? Managers should spend more of their time on long- rather than short-term payoff activities.

I recently conducted a study examining managers' behaviour in one department of a large company. I was surprised to find that only 2 per cent of their time was actually allocated to long-term strategic issues. They spent too much time firefighting, trying to solve yesterday's problems. Soon the time would come when these managers would spend all their time this way and fail to see the opportunities and possible problems of tomorrow. Should this condition be allowed to go on for too long, the consequences could be serious. Instead of firefighting being an irregular occurrence, it would become a way of life!

Companies do not last long in the market place if their management team does not pay constant vigilant attention to changing forces, forecasting, planning and taking action to correct or prevent big problems occurring.

Spending too much time on the routine

Do you spend too much time on routine tasks? Routine work is work that has a clear and precise outcome. The nature of routine work is often based upon keeping a system in action, be it computer-based or administrative. It is easy to spend all one's time feeding the system. Managers should spend time *preventing* errors occurring, rather than just processing the routine.

Do you prefer to do jobs yourself?

This is a common problem which is based upon the lack of trust. Many claim that they would give work to staff if they were sufficiently trained. Delegation is a process in which a learner is trained to work within certain guidelines.

I don't have the time!

Some managers claim they never have the time to think through all the issues, communicate their expectations to staff, and train their staff to do certain tasks. This is clearly ludicrous. They are making an excuse for not maximizing their resources. *They can find ten reasons for making a proposal fail, but not one to support it!*

If these managers would just take the time to think through the advantages of showing staff how to do work in a set way, that investment in time would pay off one hundred times because staff could *always* do that work or task. They would need no more than general support and supervision. The manager would be free to involve himself in the really important work. An initial investment, first in planning and clarifying objectives, then discussing them with staff, and training and giving support, is what separates the effective from the poor manager.

Have you clarified your criteria for delegation?

Will you delegate all the routine and monotonous work? There is danger if you do, because you may have confused 'boring' with 'low priority'. Not all the work that is high priority is interesting, rewarding and satisfying. Much of it may be routine in nature.

Take, for example, supplying routine information for a computer system. A great deal of work may be routine and predictable, but if you delegate the work, can you be sure that the person now in charge has the experience, the judgement and the skills to know when things are going wrong?

You must sit down and think through your key result areas.

- Which tasks can you delegate, and why?
- Do you want to expose others to useful learning experiences? How will you do this?
- Is there a member of staff you wish to train to take over certain responsibilities?
- Do you wish to delegate some of your time-consuming work which contributes little to your key result areas?
- Do you wish to delegate a task to the level and the person who is most able to deal with the matter in an efficient and speedy manner?
- Do you want to ensure that problems are solved as near the problem as possible?

All these questions have one thing in common. Each is a reason for delegation. The manager asks himself why he wants to delegate the work. Deciding upon the criteria for delegation is essential, if delegation is to mean more than 'just giving work to others'.

How do we delegate?

The first thing we have to do is to start trusting others. One of the major problems which face managers is that they have little faith in their staff. Can they really be trusted with the important work? Although managers know that if they took the time to train, coach and develop their staff they would achieve results, would they really be prepared to take the *risk*, letting their staff loose on the task?

This lack of confidence permeates many organizations, and the reason underlying what, in some circumstances, can become a dominant management style, is that the organization breeds managers who are averse to risk.

Risk is a factor which prevents many managers taking the initiative. They use risk as an excuse for non-performance. Risk aversion creates procrastination. Managers should learn to take 'risks' in order to develop. If they plan, plan, and plan again, the risk is minimized because all eventualities have been assessed.

So why not change from 'risk aversion' to 'planned risk'? I am not talking about delegating the high priority work which should clearly stay with the manager, but the tasks where managers have traditionally 'covered their backsides' by doing the work themselves. Think through the question, 'What is the best use of my time right now?'

What action do we need to take to delegate?

Now that the attitude towards delegation is right, and we understand the benefits of delegation, it is appropriate to look at a step-by-step approach which helps managers become more proficient at it.

The three-step approach

Step 1: Think!

First of all, think about the nature of your job. You will have already spent some time identifying your key result areas. Within these areas, isolate the tasks that you would ideally like to delegate. Think over the *criteria* for delegation. Do you want to delegate to get rid of time-consuming work which contributes little, or because you wish to coach staff, or change your key responsibilities?

Think over your tasks and identify your responsibilities. Relate responsibilities to precise and specific tasks. Now that you are aware of your priorities, ensure that your boss is fully aware of your responsibilities. This might sound strange, but there have been many instances when a senior manager's perception and the reality of work done by a subordinate bore no resemblance. It is a worthwhile experience to feed back your key priorities to your manager. It ensures that you are both rowing the boat in the same direction.

The worst thing you can do is delegate work and then find that your boss undelegates it because of issues you have not seen and discussed. So be careful.

Ensure that you involve your staff and educate them in what you have identified as key results. Are they really aware of your priorities? They may have a good idea of the tasks which you perform each day, but have they been able to relate these to the wider picture? Do they enjoy the strategic overview which you might take for granted? Have they ever had an opportunity to question you about your key result areas?

We all tend to make assumptions about the obvious. Spare the time to sit down with a few of your staff and ask them to write down their ideas of what you have to achieve each month. What are your key results? Did they get them right? Did all staff rank them in the right order of priority? How far was their perception of what you do divorced from what you actually do? Why?

If a large discrepancy exists, there is clearly a major problem. Its root does not lie just in communication but also in control. If staff's perception of your key results does not tally with yours, can you be sure that you have the cohesive management team you thought you had? How long has this situation existed and what action can you take to rectify it?

Decide on your priorities in clear, concise terms. Try to ensure that the objectives which you will delegate are achievable, realistic and measurable, otherwise how will you know if staff have made progress?

Avoid giving out instructions that are too broad, unclear, ambiguous and woolly. It is not fair on your staff. They cannot win. They need some idea of what the work will look like when it is completed, the impact it will have on them and the organization, and whether or not it meets your needs.

Plan, plan, plan and plan again

Many managers complain when staff do not achieve the targets set for them. The reason for failure can lie in the lack of personal drive and motivation of the employee, but it could lie equally well with the manager. Have you ensured that you have taken all necessary steps to ensure that your staff will succeed in achieving their targets? Nothing succeeds like success!

A positive climate of motivation and enthusiasm for work can be generated through the liberal use of rewards and praise. Obviously, staff can only be praised for consistently achieving results. If the actions for positive motivation are taken seriously by all managers, it is possible, in a short time, to develop an enthusiasm that is infectious. Success breeds success. What we all fail to do is praise!

Catch them doing something right

Think how many times we have commented on the performance of staff over the year. If you think back you will probably recollect the times when people did something *wrong*. How easy it is to comment and criticize in a negative manner. But how easy is it to catch people doing something *right* and praise their efforts? We should spend more time using praise as a positive tool of motivation and less time just being negative and critical.

Step 2: Communication

Now that your key results are agreed, you have to go further than simply communicating them to your staff. You have to communicate, in fine detail, the work, the expected results and the benefits of doing the work in a certain way.

Step 3: Taking action

When you delegate work take into account the following points.

- You must ensure that both you and your staff are aware of the rationale behind the work which they do. Why are they doing it? What are the benefits to you? Have these been expressed and communicated?
- When you do communicate with your staff, ensure that you have the opportunity to give *feedback* on their progress, and that they are aware of, and committed to, agreed completion dates. The completion dates should relate to each stage of the project, *not* just the final stage. Spotting problems early on can help you and your staff reframe your thoughts.
- When you give your staff the necessary *authority* for doing a job, ensure that you inform others of your decision, especially those who will be most affected by the delegated work. This is a valid communication exercise. Failure to inform all who are involved creates tension, conflict and bad feelings.
- When you delegate, make sure that you set personal 'degrees of freedom' for your staff. Are your staff aware of when they can proceed with work without consultation with you? Are they aware of special limiting circumstances which may arise from time to time, which require advice or support from yourself?

    Delegation is an opportunity to develop and shape the skills of people, but you can give too much at once and create a great deal of negative anxiety and stress for your staff members. Ensure that if something does go badly wrong your staff are aware of when they should seek specialist advice.

    Some managers would say, 'It has been delegated. If they hit a big problem, let them have a go and tackle it themselves. They will learn fast'. This might be the case, but what happens if things do go badly wrong?

    You have been responsible for thinking through the key issues before giving out the task. The *responsibility* for delegated tasks can never be given to others. Although you give the *authority* to do tasks, the responsibility for their completion rests with you. Do not forget this, and you will not make too many mistakes.

- When you give freedom to staff, make sure that you limit the action they can take within fairly wide parameters. But within these parameters, ensure that they have enough 'space' to use their skills and experience, that some room is left for careful experimentation and that the task is structured in such a way that it enables them to employ their creative resources.
- When staff take over the task, they accept responsibility for *their* actions. This should encourage them to think carefully through the major issues, and plan to avoid risk of failure.
- Finally, the last point to mention is that you should appraise your staff's progress at regular intervals, and give feedback as soon as possible after the completion of tasks.

One of the major savings to managers who wish to make the best use of their time is the ability to delegate wisely and to know how and when to get the most out of people. Following the basic structure of delegation, helps managers at all levels, by freeing them for more important high priority work.

Chapter 14

Problem solving

Managers spend a great deal of their time thinking through issues and trying to solve problems. That is what they are employed to do. Their ability to think clearly and solve problems in a systematic way is what differentiates them from their less effective counterparts. Managers who cannot solve problems quickly are those who either lack the talent and knowledge, or the motivation, to do so.

Those lacking in knowledge and expertise are not too much of a problem. It is possible to train managers in problem solving in a relatively short time. The motivational problem, though, is much more difficult. If a manager possesses the skills, but lacks the motivation to use them, he may well be exhibiting signs of *procrastination* (see Chapter 6). Perhaps he has little idea of target setting or goal planning, or perhaps he is just disorganized!

Whatever the cause, the effect is the same: problems remain problems and no action is taken to right what is wrong. Why is it that so many managers put off what they should be doing? Are they afraid of taking risks, or do they fear failure?

Procrastination, or fear of putting a solution to a problem, can be a big time waster. But what can we do about it, and what action should we take?

Problem solving and decision making

First of all, do not try to compartmentalize these two areas. They are not discrete. They overlap. You can attend a meeting and start applying the 'problem solving' process to a particular issue, but if you are not careful, you will find others making *decisions* before the cause of the problem has been identified!

We can all jump to conclusions, make unreal assumptions and peddle our latest pet solution, all in aid of saving time. We may do so in the short term, e.g. dealing with an agenda quickly, but will we have solved the problem once and for all? I doubt it. We may be so concerned with shortening the time allowed for the discussion that we do not solve the problem. In fact, we create further problems for ourselves, because we have not got it 'right first time'.

How can we avoid jumping to the wrong conclusion?

Sit down and think over the main issues. How do you normally solve problems? Do you debate at length and then vote? If that is the case, the decision is not based upon consensus, and it is likely that the decision reached will not have been gleaned from the whole range of alternatives.

Do you automatically think there is one right answer? This might well be the case when dealing with accounts, production schedules, etc., but most problems do not have one solution, they have many! What you have got to do is plan your resources to consider the best options.

Problem solving – the logical approach

When we think of problem solving, we tend to examine a logical approach to understanding the underlying causes of problems. Then we decide to tackle the problems in a number of steps (see Fig. 14.1). This is the way we think about a problem, but how often do we really think through the key stages and activities which we need to pursue in order to find a right answer?

Stage 1: Problem definition

The *real* cause of the problem may be the inherent nature of the job itself. It may lack interest and satisfaction, or the supervisor may be creating difficulty. Whatever the cause, we shall never know, if we have gone for the easy option, and dealt with the effect of the problem rather than with the cause. The underlying difficulty still exists and will manifest itself in other ways. We have dealt with the effect!

Many management problems are never solved because we adopt this logical approach. For example, the way to increase productivity in an ailing plant may seem to be to run a redundancy programme. It may be decided that the criterion used for redundancy will be length of service with the company, in other words 'last in first out'. There is no mention

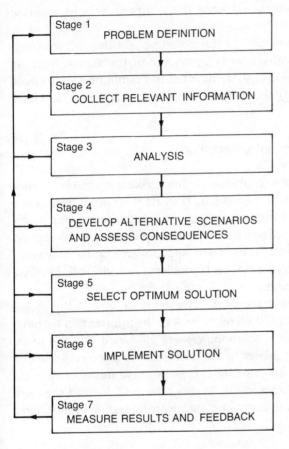

Fig. 14.1 *Logical approach to problem solving*

of keeping the most able and getting rid of the least able!

We appear to have solved the problem on the surface. We have reduced manpower, but will this increase productivity? What we should have done was to look at the contributory cause of the problem and examine manpower resourcing strategies. Jumping to the easy, quick-fix solution does not pay off in the long term.

Avoid the option of least resistance

The above is a situation where management decide to pursue the option that gives least resistance, rather than pursuing the line that is in the long-term interests of the company.

I know of a company who could not afford the luxury of a personnel manager, but nevertheless appointed one at great expense because the line managers would not take responsibility for personnel matters. The company was only small and personnel matters could have been dealt with by line managers, certainly until the company was in a better financial position.

Failing to identify the nature of the problem, and dealing with the effects rather than the causes, is symptomatic of problem solving in many organizations. However, time devoted to examining cause–effect relationships, and defining the full parameters of a problem, is time well spent.

Stage 2: Collecting relevant information

Some managers try to solve problems without asking themselves what information they need to do a good job. They let their prejudices guide their judgement., They let their preferences structure the solution. Even worse, they have a kitbag of solutions which are just ready to be applied to problems, whether or not they are appropriate! Some managers spend all their lives 'trying to find problems which will fit their solutions'. Do not join them.

The classic mistake we make is that we tend to look at the broad parameters of a problem and then relate back to the information we have that will help us produce a solution. We are all aware that the more information we have that relates to the problem, the more accurate our diagnosis will be. Some, unfortunately, make a grave mistake. They do not look at the information and ask 'Is this relevant?' Instead they say 'How can I use it?' They are confusing *available* information with *required* information (see Fig. 14.2).

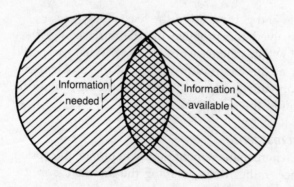

Fig. 14.2 Solving problems with the information required

How easy it is to use all the information you have collected, rather than that which you really need to solve the problem! From my lecturing days, I remember students filling their dissertations with vast quantities of data which they never used or referred to in their theses. They stored the information and included it in the appendices because it made them feel warm and comfortable and gave them some security. The information was of no value. It added nothing. It certainly did not add *value* to the recommendations. Instead it detracted and took away any credibility.

This same problem is illustrated in too many management reports. Quantities of data are appended, not to add weight to the quality of the research, but, often, for reasons connected with the author's image.

Collecting too much
A problem that many experience is collecting too much information, but failing to have any regard for *quality*. They confuse the two and feel that *quantity* can be traded for quality! It never can be. Quantity is no substitute for quality.

Measuring everything and understanding nothing
Some people display a compulsion to measure everything that can be measured, and neglect other important variables which may not be so easily measured. These may be important, but they are neglected, and this can lead to inaccuracies in problem resolution. Collecting vast quantities of data is somehow reassuring; whether the information will be of practical use does not seem quite so important a consideration.

Stage 3: Analysis

We all tend to make too many assumptions. Many of these 'assumptions' are based upon our own many and varied experiences in a given situation. We can generalize but this creates problems. The worst area of generalization is when we make assumptions between *cause* and *effect*. For example, a company may experience a decrease in sales, and have industrial relations problems at the same time.

Did the IR situation lead to decreased sales, or did they have something to do with a drop in consumer expenditure, shoddy products or poor customer relations? We may never know. But what we must be wary of is jumping to assumptions which reinforce our prejudices!

When analysing cause–effect relationships, ensure that there are no significant intervening variables. Joan Woodward's research into organization structures in the 1950s is a case in point. Woodward was trying to establish the degree to which there was a relationship between companies who practised and adhered to some of the 'classical principles of management' and their success. The research was undertaken in 100 companies in the South East of England. The conclusions suggested that no such relationship existed!

Was there a direct relationship? Did those companies who practised certain management principles reap their rewards with commercial success? Surely, the researchers thought, there must be some relationship? There was, but it took quite some time to find. There was an intervening variable which explained the complicated nature of the relationship.

It was *technology*. The technology employed by the company, e.g. process, mass production, craft, etc., was a determining factor that gave a full explanation to the research findings. Without the missing link between cause and effect there was no meaningful explanation at all.

Be aware that all the facts will not 'jump out' at you all at once. You may need to pursue other lines of enquiry to establish *intervening* factors. Be careful and do not make too many *assumptions*.

Stage 4: Develop alternative scenarios and assess consequences

While working through the analysis phase and establishing cause and effect relationships, remember you are not looking for 'one right answer'. Hopefully, you will develop a number of options which should help you to achieve your goal. If you go for the 'one right answer', you may be neglecting other strategies which will have payoffs for you.

Before you dive in, think through a number of scenarios, and assess the consequences of each strategy. Think of the benefits in the short, and the long, term. Think through the disadvantages and the costs of the action. Then, progress to the next stage.

Stage 5: Select the optimum solution

At this stage problem solving and decision making merge. Perhaps the forming of a group of managers, or a formal meeting, will be required in order to achieve the optimum solution. This will require the skills of meetings management. (See Chapters 8 and 9.) Involve those who are to be most affected by any change. If they have to live with the solution and put it into practice, surely they have to play a part in contributing to the overall approach and finer details?

Stage 6: Implement solution and create change

This is one of the most difficult stages in problem solving and requires more *action* than words. Solutions, when written on paper, seem to work fine, but when implemented, can create all sorts of problems.

Most of these are human in origin, and require new ways of working. 'Change' can create resistance. It is worth considering the 'people problems' before implementing new ideas. Ask yourself, 'In how many ways can this idea fail?' Address the doubts you raise, and be prepared to take corrective action.

Remember, we only achieve results through others. However good the idea generated by yourself and colleagues, if staff will not put it into practice and accept the solution or innovation, your solution will *remain* a good idea and never become a reality!

Stage 7: Monitor and measure results and gain feedback

It is all very well creating change and moving on to the next problem. To ensure that you got it 'right first time', gain feedback on the practicality of the solution which has been implemented. Seek the views of those people who are most affected by your 'solution'. Their feedback is an important element in the problem solving and decision making process. Without their consent and input, how can you hope to win their support to implement your solution?

Alternative problem solving techniques – creative approaches

We have referred to the logical, sequential approach to the solution of problems, but have paid little attention to the more creative approach. Creative thinking and brainstorming are approaches that have helped many companies solve complex problems. These alternative approaches are particularly useful when there is no one right answer.

There may be a variety of answers 'close together', or one right answer to production, accounting or engineering problems. Using the same approach for open-ended problems can be disastrous. You will spend a tremendous amount of *time* trying to find the one right way to solve them. It does not exist, so why look for it!

Let us look at more creative problem solving techniques and examine their applicability to management problem solving. First, the creative techniques tend to be used more frequently in areas which involve human resources and marketing. The methods to increase productivity, quality and image are various.

Brainstorming and *cause–effect analysis* have helped particularly in quality improvement and initiatives, where those who produce a component meet together and 'solve' a production or quality problem. The *quality circles* approach to improving product quality relies on these creative approaches to problem solving.

What is creative thinking?

Creative thinking is 'relating those things which were previously unrelated'. This means that the mind has to freewheel and overcome the self-imposed barriers which can stop us moving towards innovative solutions. Edward De Bono, in particular, has spent many years teaching his variant of the creative approach to problem solution called 'lateral thinking'. His thoughts on creative strategies which others use to achieve and meet their targets are well documented in *Tactics*.

Creative thinking is concerned with developing innovative solutions to traditional problems. It is also a set of techniques orientated towards extracting a large number of ideas from a group of people.

Brainstorming

The first step in using the brainstorming technique is to define the nature of the problem, and express it in one statement. For instance, let us assume that productivity in a manufacturing department is falling. We may define the problem thus: 'In how many ways can we increase productivity in the department?'

Do not jump at this statement, because we are unsure whether we are really dealing with the overall problem. What we need to do is develop *restatements* of the problem, e.g.

'In how many ways can we increase group activity?'

'In how many ways can we reduce unnecessary costs?'

'What action can we take to ensure we always manufacture high quality goods?'

'What manpower strategies can we use to ensure that both satisfaction and productivity remain high?'

Clearly, you can make as many restatements as you wish, but the overall purpose is to walk around the problem and look at it from different angles. This is most important. Otherwise, we tend to pursue the old tried and tested techniques.

Having a group of managers restate the problem in ten or twelve restatements is the first stage of a good problem solving workshop. The next activity is to agree the work in one 'restatement'.

Freewheeling

Think of a trivial problem that faces you all and get the group to brainstorm ideas quickly. You are not yet concerned with solving the problem, but rather with giving those attending the confidence to develop new ideas, however wild!

Rules

The rules for brainstorming include:

1. Do not try to find one right answer. It does not exist. There are many answers which might be of use.
2. Build confidence among the team and stress that they should try to generate as many ideas as possible. These ideas must not be evaluated, but listed, to be discussed later. Do not evaluate, otherwise a lot of good ideas will never be expressed.
3. Avoid tunnel vision. Think through areas to take the group away from established practice. Do not let them dwell too much on old solutions.
4. Reduce the capacity of members to analyse suggestions too quickly. They must avoid statements like 'That will not work' or 'We tried that at my last company and found it to be too expensive.' Evaluation is left for later. At the moment, the key activity is the generation of ideas.
5. Many managers attending brainstorming sessions feel uncomfortable; they fear looking foolish and so do not contribute. You must break down any barriers and encourage ideas, however zany they appear!

Agreeing criteria for evaluation

Now that the brainstorming session is over, the group have to get together to agree criteria by which they will judge their ideas. Once criteria are agreed, e.g. cost, administrative convenience, long-term impact, economical and technical feasibility, etc., it is comparatively easy to evaluate your *list* of ideas.

Logical structure

Here we move away from *divergent* to *convergent* thinking, where you evaluate the brainstormed proposals. This is the process you would normally go through if you always used the rational method of problem solving, except that you now have lots of creative ideas to evaluate.

This approach helps you develop new, innovative approaches to solving problems which may have existed for too long.

Cause–effect analysis

This technique is used a great deal by teams of workers and staff involved in quality improvement initiatives. The technique has a logical structure and framework which is easily understood, and it incorporates elements of creative thought.

Cause–effect analysis is a good, simple technique for examining the major factors which *impact* upon a particular problem (see Fig. 14.3). There are two stages in this analysis.

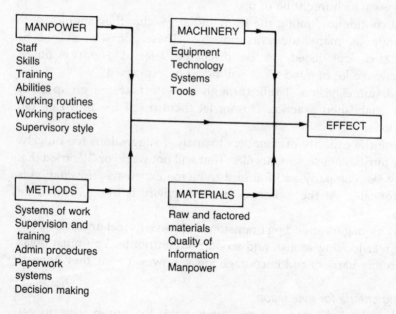

Fig. 14.3 Cause–effect analysis (the fishbone diagram)

Stage 1

Define the symptoms of the problem. What is the *effect* on staff, the department and the organization? Describe this effect in detail. List the consequences. Walk around the problem and consider it from different angles.

Stage 2
This requires a skilful eye, an intelligent mind, and a commitment to identifying all factors that can contribute to the effects of the problem.

A team of staff should get together to brainstorm the possible and probable causes of the problem. Brainstorming and listing *causes* should be related to the '4Ms'.

The 4Ms
The '4Ms' is a simple and convenient method for isolating the probable causes of a problem under four headings:

- *Manpower* – includes staff skills, training, abilities, attitudes, working routines and practices;
- *Methods* – includes systems of work, paperwork routines, etc.;
- *Machinery* – includes equipment, technology, systems, etc.;
- *Materials* – includes raw and factored materials, statistics, information, etc.

Brainstorm and generate a list of all the possible factors which could create the *effect*. Generate long lists, and do not evaluate them as you write them down.

After you have listed the *probable causes,* you will be able to add them to your own *fishbone diagram.* You should then isolate key areas for investigation, agree targets and review dates.

Using the fishbone diagram will not, by itself, solve the problem, but it will help you examine the interrelationships between the 4Ms and give you sufficient information on which you can then base appropriate action.

Taking action

Do not assume that the problem solving techniques, by themselves, will solve all your problems. They will not. They will, however, give you a basis on which you can make a balanced decision.

If a problem has existed for a long time, do not assume that you can create action to solve the problem 'right first time'. You will have to consider the steps you should take in the short, immediate and the long term.

The approach you adopt will be determined by the urgency of putting right what is wrong, the resources you have at your disposal, and the degree to which you require instant results.

Corrective action

This is solving a problem after it has arisen. Going back and carrying out rework may fix the problem in the short term, but will not remove the cause. In other words, firefighting might be an effective short-term strategy, but it is not a substitute for *right first time.*

Preventative action

This is the best approach to problem solving. Time, energy, effort and enthusiasm devoted to *preventing* problems arising is well spent. Remember, one hour of planning can save ten hours of chaos (see Chapter 5).

Although problem solving and decision making are inextricably linked, we may ask how should we organize our time to make the best quality decisions. First of all, we should look at the decisions we have to make, and use our daily planner to assess whether they are important in the *long, medium* or *short* term.

We must also look at the decisions and ask ourselves whether they are complex or routine. Routine decisions can be delegated to others (see Chapter 13). You yourself have to deal with the more difficult ones. Usually decisions are difficult to make because you lack the necessary information to act in the best interests of everyone. As the decisions become more difficult, as the solutions to the problems become more complex, you will need the support of other people. They will give you different perspectives and information which you do not possess. It is appropriate that you adopt a managerial style that is suited to solving the problem based upon the resources at hand.

This means that your 'man management' skills will be brought into play, and your ability to manage meetings (see Chapters 8 and 9) will be required in order to get the best out of people. Think over the criteria by which others will judge your decisions and, if in doubt, remember that *planning* is the best way of ensuring that errors do not arise.

Problem solving and decision making are subjects which occupy much of a manager's time. Henry Minzberg identified *decision making* as one of those things on which managers spend a great deal of time.

Understanding the logical, and the creative, approaches to problem solving will help many to save time and make quality decisions.

Chapter 15

Managing your stress

Stress is probably the biggest problem that managers have to face at work. Stress is intangible, it cannot be seen, only experienced. Stress does not exist, yet many people each year have to take time off from work to resolve the conflicts and tensions in their life. Stress is the twentieth century disease and the biggest and most significant time waster of all.

Before we start examining the negative elements of stress, let us look at the positive side. We all do need some degree of stress. It is stress that spurs us on to achieve. If we experienced no stress at all, there would be no drive or stimulation to do anything. However, if we have drive to do a job, we do so because we value the reward for completing the task. As our perception of stress intensifies, so we are forced to act to complete certain tasks. In fact, we can see that there is a direct relationship between stress and performance – see Fig. 15.1. The diagram illustrates that, as we experience greater stress or tension, this acts as a motivator to perform and achieve a set goal. However, there comes a time when the stress becomes too great and we cannot cope with any further increase. This then influences our performance. Thus stress overload reduces our capacity to perform, and we find that our effectiveness declines rapidly.

As stated previously, the presence of stress can, in normal circumstances, be a great motivator, but we have to try and ensure that it does not become too great, and create situations where we are so 'stimulated' and agitated that we perform poorly.

Understanding stress

What causes stress?

There is no one cause, but you can guess who is behind it. You yourself are! Stress does not exist naturally, it is an intangible pressure or strain

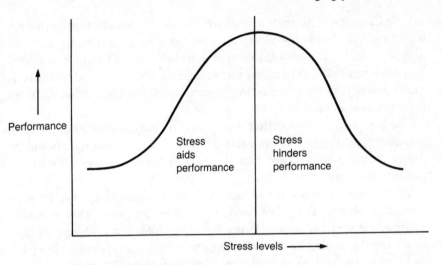

Fig. 15.1 Relationship between stress and performance

which can act as a spur for some people yet create severe problems for others.

Your response to stress

Stress for one man is challenge, stimulation and excitement, for another, it may mean anxiety, conflict, tension and fear. Stress is determined by how we approach it. If we think that an event will be stressful, it will be. If we feel that stress is necessary to create the required arousal to succeed at a particular task, we are using stress in a positive manner. Stress is neither good nor bad, it is our response to it that makes it either a negative, or positive, force.

Worry

A great many people worry about all manner of things. Certain circumstances are in themselves anxiety provoking and create worry. When this worry expands out of all proportion it can start having a negative influence on our effectiveness. Research into the sorts of things which people worry about suggests that 40 per cent of these things never happened, 35 per cent were things which could not be changed, 15 per cent turned out to be better than expected, 8 per cent were trivial and only 2 per cent were legitimate worries.

This research puts things in perspective. Perhaps the next time we start worrying we can remember it and not get so wound up in ourselves!

Dale Carnegie recommends that we allocate 10–20 minutes per day for worrying. We should not worry outside this time! So if something preys on your mind, tell yourself to forget it and allocate it to the 20 minutes you have put aside. When you are successful, you will see that worry is more a state of mind, reflecting your outlook on life, rather than an objective assessment of reality.

The logic behind this is that we could too easily spend all day letting something prey on our mind and distract us from what we should be doing. Some people claim that they are natural worriers. 'It's in my nature', they say.

When one problem clears up, they find something else to start worrying about. They are wrong in their attitude. This negative approach is very hindering. Every time they look at a problem, all they see is the dark side, the fear, the anxiety, conflict and tension. They fail to be positive, and have confidence in themselves. They should focus their attention on the good things in a situation, and then work on making these happen. They should not dwell on the negative side, taking themselves further and further into a negative depression.

Who suffers most from stress?

There are many myths about stress. Too many believe that it is only senior executives who qualify to experience stress. Research suggests that labourers experience more stress than some of our senior executives. Research into Swedish heart attack victims has shown that it is not the high powered executive who's most at risk, but the employee with the boring routine job. A monotonous job with little opportunity to learn new skills increases the heart attack risk by 40 per cent. People in jobs that are monotonous, but also hectic, fare even worse with nearly 60 per cent greater risk. Even irregular hours seem to be a high risk factor, with adverse effects from night shift work on blood pressure, and adrenalin and fat levels. Those who fall into the low risk category are those who work regular hours at a reasonable pace with plenty of opportunity to use skill, initiative and responsibility.

Senior staff at least have the power to influence their environment! They may have to deal with conflicts and ambiguity, but in most situations they can change their environment to make it more comfortable.

The unskilled worker has little discretion or power over the work he performs. He will have to react continually to instructions and conditions which many others would find intolerable. The nature of some non-skilled jobs is routine and repetitive and gives little scope for psychological growth, responsibility, satisfaction or self-esteem.

Change

The impact of change, especially on workers in declining industries, is severe. In recent years we have witnessed the death of many traditional industries and the impact this has had on local communities and family life.

The unemployed suffer their own particular variant of stress and tension. Maslow proposes that one of man's basic needs is to provide himself with shelter and protect himself against the contingencies of the future. According to Maslow's hierarchy of needs (see Fig. 15.2) this satisfaction can be measured by the degree to which we progress up the hierarchy. Extending and going beyond the most basic to the higher order needs is what can contribute to satisfaction in our lives. For the unemployed, it is difficult to fulfil needs at even the basic level. This will create conflict and tension because they lack the means by which they

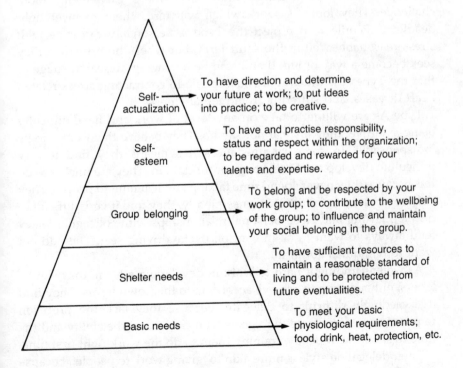

Fig. 15.2 Maslow and need satisfaction

can meet even their lowest order requirements, thus it is impossible, in Maslow's view, for them even to attempt to meet higher order needs.

Personality types

Type A

You have no doubt heard of the terms Type A and Type B personality. The Type A is the go-getter, the high achiever. He is the one who responds readily to situations, and who tends to express anger and aggression at the least provocation. He is the person who looks for the shortest queue at the supermarket checkout, and then loses his temper because the queue is not moving as fast as the others!

If we tend to function at the level of Type A behaviour all the time, it can lead to chronic tension and stress overload. If we are constantly wound up, like a tense spring, sooner or later this will lead to a deterioration in our health.

Some Type A personalities crave ever more excitement, more challenge. They look for work which will force them to meet tight deadlines. People who project the Type A personality can cope with stress reasonably well in the short term, but when the pressures they seek become a way of life, then it can be damaging. Research suggests that the Type A is much more susceptible to contracting stress related heart diseases, and suffering from mental illness.

Type As are willing to take on any level of work and have difficulty being assertive, they just cannot say no! They believe themselves to be indispensable. In some circumstances this means they find it very difficult to develop a cohesive team around them. They are unable to do this because they never spend time talking and listening to people. They only communicate for action. Consequently, they find it very difficult to develop lasting and close personal relationships with colleagues. They tend always to want to be in control, in the driving seat. They do not want to relinquish authority.

As well as finding it hard to work in developing a team, they can be loners, only wishing to achieve according to their own terms. They find it exceedingly difficult to delegate, because they lack the precision required to communicate their goals with clarity and the ability and the time to spend with people training them to do the work right first time.

Their delegation style is more akin to 'giving work to people', because they themselves lack the specific expertise to complete it. They think that others should show the same urgency in the work they do. They cannot understand those who do not show the same commitment.

Type As are driven by challenge and urgency. Their style of work is characterized by the 'urgent' taking over from the 'important'. Although they can do a number of projects at the same time, the quality of their work is sometimes lessened because they have never allowed enough time to think through the key issues to the level needed to do a good job.

Planning tends to be haphazard. Type As tend not to prioritize their goals. Their goals are pursued on the basis of first come, first served. Consequently, if – and when – they fail, they do it in style!

Type B

Those of the Type B personality do not have the same aggressive drive for achievement and success, but their life style does more to protect them in the long term. Type As manufacture their own tension and conflict by creating unrealistic demands and constraints on their time. Type Bs tend to under-achieve, finding it difficult sometimes to develop the internal drive necessary to stir them into action.

In some circumstances, this can weigh against them because they tend to depend too heavily on past achievements, forgetting that these have little reference to today. As Type As manufacture pressure to meet deadlines, so Type Bs find it difficult to motivate themselves. To succeed, Type Bs have to set deadlines and work to them rigidly!

Like Type As, Bs find it difficult to prioritize and set goals that have meaning and will stretch their abilities. They tend not to have balance. Many Bs tend to force themselves to the point of perfection trying to get something 100 per cent right, even when the value of the work is negligible.

Best of both worlds

What we require is a mix of a 'healthy balance' between the two styles. If you exhibit the frenzied characteristics of the Type A manager, isn't it time that you cooled down and took a fresh look at the problems you face. Force yourself to step back from your work and identify the key priorities and tasks you wish to perform. Look around you at the talent in your management team and in the organization as a whole, and remember that the worth of a manager is not measured by what he can achieve, but what he gets others to achieve!

Use the strengths of your team and delegate to the right level. Do not 'jump' at problems; think about their causes and the consequences of several courses of action. Do not grab at one solution and force it to work. Most important of all, you will have to plan ahead to ensure that time restrictions do not force you back into your old ways! Using the daily planner and apportioning time to work you 'must', 'should' and 'like' to do, should help you avoid the chaos of your previous life style. Don't forget, the biggest problem Type As have is saying 'no'! For some reason they like taking on additional work!

If you exhibit Type B behaviour you have to start setting yourself goals with deadlines and sub-targets by which you can measure your performance. Your main problem will be self-motivation, so you will have to examine the structure of rewards which will really motivate you to achieve. You must not become bogged down in detail, but adopt more of an overview, and relate the effort you put into the work to the relative importance of the output.

Some Type Bs spend too much time and energy on things they like to do and no time at all on things which have little interest for them!

Clearly, what we want to achieve is a combination of the 'positive' sides of A and B behaviour. Ideally, we would like to combine the personal orientation and the group working of the B category, with the high achieving, deadline setting of the A type. The attention to detail of the Type B, coupled with the volume of work consumed by the Type A would improve performance all around.

It is unlikely that you will exhibit the extreme behaviour of either A or B, but you should be able to recognize your behaviour and take action to ensure that stress does not get the better of you!

Coping with stress

Stress as a major cause of productive time lost will never be identified in the statistics in the *Employment Gazette*, but stress can be the major factor *behind* the big productivity losses each year. In recent years it has been estimated that 10 million working days were lost as a result of industrial accidents. Smoking related diseases accounted for another 10 million and a further 10 million days were lost because of alcoholism. These figures represent a tremendous waste. We should examine the underlying cause of 'productive days lost'. It is pretty obvious that the factors behind many of the problems are stress related.

If we examine alcoholism as a major problem, we can find that there are other causes which distract people from their work and their family life and make them alcoholics. There are no agreed causal links, but certainly a great deal of stress, strain and tension at work can create the situation where alcohol may be used as a stimulant or as a depressant to help the individual unwind from the anxieties of life. Once alcohol takes hold it leads to a condition where the individual becomes psychologically and, eventually, physically dependent upon the drug. Alcohol can help reduce the symptoms of stress in the short term, but when its use and abuse take over and become the individual's major method of coping with stress, that is when it can become a real time and life waster!

Work may not be the cause of the stress or tension which leads to alcoholism. There can be many other deep-seated problems which may account for the condition. However, the effect is witnessed at work and creates many problems. Some companies have recognized that they can help employees and have created campaigns and programmes to this end.

A large manufacturing company has recently pursued a 'Live for Life' programme concerned with promoting individual and organizational health through a number of media. Fitness and diet is one strand of the drive, but sport and yoga are also included. A large number of employees attend the various events, seeking to prevent the dysfunctions associated with stress and related conditions.

An interesting point to note is that some staff attending the programme have strange views about stress! Some comments overheard include, 'I am surprised to see you here, I didn't know you were stressed', or 'I do not need to go to those sessions, I don't suffer from stress'. Some staff do not seem to realize that the programme is not necessarily corrective or remedial in nature. It has not been designed to 'get you back on your feet', rather it is preventative and educational.

Knowing how to cope with change, stress and tension, not just in your work, but also your family life, can add many pleasant years to your life and eradicate a great deal of time-wasting anxiety!

Some researchers suggest that work, although a central life *activity*, may not be a central life *interest* for everybody. Although we agree that work can be too much of a life interest for many managers, this is not true for everyone. Many employees do not get from their work the 'buzz' that gives others the psychological reward and satisfaction. Researchers suggest that some work, especially that which is monotonous, routine or boring, can have an impact that manifests itself in 'days lost' through absenteeism and uncertificated absence. The nature of the work itself can be alienating, leading, in many instances, to severe problems. A great deal of research in the 1960s and 1970s suggests that the inherent nature and satisfaction of a job can influence the well-being and self-worth of the person doing that job. In some circumstances, this can lead to depression and mental illness.

Stress management

What should we do about alienation?

Many companies have decided to restructure and redesign work around the needs of people, not just the demands of the job. This means throwing away traditional ideas on the 'division of labour' as the principle underlying job design and examining issues pertinent to building and designing satisfaction and psychological reward into the job at every stage.

How does stress affect our performance?

Quite easily. However well we plan we must be aware that contingencies arise and that we have to respond immediately. This means that we have to adopt a flexible style to planning:

'If anything can go wrong it will; everything takes longer than you think; and we always seem to underestimate difficulties' (Murphy's Law)

If we always take account of Murphy's Law we can take action to ensure that not too many problems arise. This means maximum flexibility. If we reject this rule and instead go ahead and plan too rigidly throughout the day, we will find that if something does happen to disturb our equilibrium, then we will be rushed to complete all our daily tasks.

Those managers who believe that time management is about making every second count throughout the day are wrong. Using a daily planner in such a way is going to create a tremendous amount of stress. One appointment can take longer than expected, and, sooner or later, the manager will find that he is behind in his work. If he were an effective manager he would take account of contingencies and then reorder or *reprioritize* his day as problems arose.

Two sides of the same coin

Time and stress management are two sides of the same coin. If you can manage and organize your time and your tasks well, decide on priorities and plan ahead, and use the resources at your disposal, you will not have any problems. However, if you are ruled by others and fail to manage your time properly, you will be stressed for no apparent reason.

Likewise, you have to be a good manager of men. On some occasions, to keep your head above water, you will have to be more assertive. If you are the sort of manager who takes everything on, beware, you could be creating a bad time for yourself in the future!

How often do you stay late at the office? Too often? If you do, are you making the most of your time? I doubt it. Many managers confuse attendance with performance. In some cases, it appears to be more important for others to see your car in the car park rather than you working!

Worse, do you feel guilty when you leave work on time? If you do you are in danger of being at work for the wrong reasons!

You must develop balance to your life, there is a limit to your effectiveness – after spending so much time at work what impact on your productivity will that extra hour or two of attendance have? Probably very little. You should make time in which to relax and unwind from the daily pressures.

Avoiding stress

- Let's admit it, there are times in your life when work is coming thick and fast. You will manage it more effectively if you can, first of all, decide on your priorities. Once these have been agreed, decide who is going to do what and when. If you have staff, use their expertise, resources and creativity to achieve your results.
- Be assertive. If you are snowed under, say so! Do not give in or feel guilty. You have rights to protect. If you take on too much work you will find that your effectiveness will decline sharply. If you take on everything you will achieve little in terms of quality.
- Be wary whether you display the characteristics of Type A or B personality. Know them. Examine the actions you can take to be more effective rather than more efficient.
- Do not procrastinate. Do not put off work you dislike doing till tomorrow. Do it now!

- Examine your deadlines. Do not get too stressed if you cannot meet them. What *will* add to your stress levels is failing to tell others that you cannot achieve the desired results by the set time. If you don't tell them, they are going to be constantly on the phone bothering you and creating even more problems. Is it not better to meet with or phone them and tell them that the work will be late? Your self-esteem may take a minor blow, but at least it is one less worry to have. If the deadline is a deadline, then you had better start reordering your priorities pretty damn quick!

- If you have difficulty doing certain types of work, or you find yourself led off to do other things, try to cut off your favourite escapes. Force yourself to work on projects for 30 minute spells and then reward yourself. The barrier that a lot of managers face is trying to do everything at once. Of course they cannot, but that does not help them cope with the anxiety and worry! You must adopt the 'little steps' approach. Lots of little steps or stages will help you achieve your goal. Often the size of the problem can distract you from focusing upon the component parts.

- Take up a sport or hobby. Everybody needs something demanding outside their work to add balance to their life. A physical sport, which induces sufficient exercise, is far preferable for burning off the aggression than participating in 'passive sports' like darts and snooker.

- Talk to others about your problems. You will find that other people will help you put your 'stress problems' in perspective. Remember, only 2 per cent of the problems that cause people worry actually come about.

- You should not take yourself too seriously. We know that seconds tick away every day, and the one thing we all have in common is that there is less time for all of us. Life is about enjoyment and balance. Some of us only realize this half way through the second week of our summer holiday!

- Use the principles of time management orientated to planning, organizing, priority setting, delegation, assertiveness and procrastination and you will find you do not have a stress problem, because you will have taken sufficient *preventative* action to eradicate the negative elements of stress.

Chapter 16

Managing your life and your career

Time management is not an obsessive desire to cram more into the day. Neither is it an attempt to make every single minute count. We don't want you dashing around in a hectic spin, trying to achieve everything in one day. I don't believe that effective managers are the sort of people who rush around imitating the 'white tornado'. If you remember, he didn't achieve much, apart from being seen dashing from office to office, flying upstairs, jumping in and out of lifts with handfuls of white paper.

I hope that you will have gained a different perspective, far removed from merely trying to cram more into the day. I hope that you have seen the light! Time management is about balance in all things. This chapter concentrates upon expanding upon some of the ideas we have discussed and planning your life the way you want to live it.

Without any doubt, time management is central to any management development activity. Time is the most important resource at hand, and once managers have learnt to use this resource, and achieve their targets, they have a good idea of managing other resources.

If managers can use their time well they must be skilled in the following areas:

- delegation;
- assertiveness;
- team building;
- motivation of self and others;
- objective setting;
- paperwork management;
- procrastination (or rather avoiding it!)
- stress management;
- meetings management;
- career and life planning.

Although the list appears endless, the most important area is the last one. That is why we are here! We might have a short-term orientation to please the boss, manage meetings well and complete our routine paperwork on time every time. But this is all geared to something much bigger, something that we take for granted and something we don't manage too well, that is *career and life planning*.

We are so busy chasing our tails, that when we do find the time to relax we sit back and do just that. Then the merry-go-round starts again and we all jump on! How many of us actually think first why we do what we do? Very few.

The obituary test

A friend of mine who used to run management development workshops would ask those attending to take part in a short exercise. The exercise required those present to think over their lives, their achievements and where they were going. He got them to write their *own obituary*!

Although this may sound strange, it made those attending the session sit up and take note. Some found it a very difficult task to complete. Others couldn't take it seriously. Others tried and were surprised. What was written down in front of them on a scrap of paper, in 50 to 100 words, was a testament to a man's life. This small fragment of paper reflected a man's hopes, needs, aspirations and achievements.

For what would *you* like to be remembered?

Confronting the reality of the 'obituary test' can be devastating. Those who take it seriously will learn. Those who fail to take it seriously are doing themselves a grave disservice.

Mid-life crisis

The experience of a colleague of mine is surely familiar to many managers. Jim was 44, happily married, with two children, both grown up. He was a professional man who seemed happy with his life. But then one day, he expressed a feeling of dissatisfaction.

I did not know if this was related to his age, although I suspect it was, but I was sure of one thing, he had been chasing career progression, material possessions and so on, but when he had time to stop, to sit down and think clearly, he wondered what he was doing with his life. He asked himself, 'Is this what I *really* want?'

The story is not new. There are many instances when people sit down and think about their past and ask 'How did I get here?' Unfortunately, many cannot answer. It has been described as 'mid-life crisis.' The solutions include drastically changing all aspects of one's life. Marriage and career are the major victims. It is the first time that many people have had the opportunity to sit down and evaluate their past and their future, both at the same time, and then make a decision about how they are going to spend the rest of their life!

What characterizes the mid-life crisis is that people look back and see that their children are now grown and starting out on their own. Usually the father or mother has risen to a responsible position at work, but finds it difficult to move up further. Relationships that have existed for perhaps two decades are questioned, and the person decides whether he or she wishes to continue life in the same manner.

The future for many is just a continuation of the past! But many decide to break with what they consider to be routine, humdrum lives and venture out anew, like a young man or woman looking at the world for the first time, looking for new experiences and outlooks, looking for something which will give meaning to their life.

More and more people are experiencing this traumatic stage in their life.

This is the first day of the rest of my life

We hear of successful businessmen who apply for jobs in nature reserves, of managers who drop out, or married men or women who seek to complete the education they were denied earlier. They join an Open University course, meeting others who have decided to reject the life they have followed up to now and start out again.

For many, this new start is a mission. Others, who are older, may look back and resent the path they have followed. They feel it is too late to make a fresh start.

Planning our life and our career

How many of us really plan our lives or our careers? Not many. A fairly standard way I start a session on career development is to ask those attending to tell me how much time, effort and energy they expend choosing:

- the accommodation in which they live;
- the holidays they go on each year;
- the vehicle they drive.

The replies I get back are amazing! People spend so much time looking for the right house, negotiating for the car they want and doing a lot of walking and talking, choosing their annual holiday.

I then ask them how much of their time they spend on planning their *career* and their *life*. There is a silence. Someone might say that they are continually thinking of their future. Others say you cannot plan it, it just happens.

Well, perhaps the latter is partly right. But only because we fail to take responsibility for making things happen! Research into career dynamics suggests that a great deal that happens to people is by chance. But those who succeed, have usually taken some time to think through their future, made some plans, and adhere to them.

Opportunity

Many argue that career progression can be a matter of the right opportunity turning up. This may be true in some circumstances, but there are still those managers who would not recognize an opportunity if they fell over it! Many fail to realize that one can *create* opportunities by pursuing a 'plan for change'.

Planning

Career development and success is a combination of a number of things. Planning is important, if for no other reason than that it educates you into recognizing how an event could be construed as an opportunity or one step which will help you get what you want.

Planning is so important because it enables you to think through the sequence of activities and events which you have to achieve before you arrive at your destination. Planning, by itself, will never achieve what you want. I know many people who are excellent planners, but never achieve any of their goals. They are unrealistic in setting their targets, don't necessarily possess the skills to achieve their goals and lack the discipline and self-motivation to make it happen!

Luck and opportunity

Luck and opportunity are also significant ingredients in career development. We all need luck. Meeting the right person, sitting next to the right manager at a meeting, having a report read by someone with influence. It may or may not happen to us. It is a matter of luck and opportunity.

What can this chapter do to help you achieve more? Do not be negative and say 'I am never lucky.' You have to make your own luck. Read Norman Vincent Peale, *You Can if You Think You Can*, or Dale Carnegie, *How to Make Friends and Influence People*. These books were written a long time ago, but the message they project is still appropriate today. Go out and create your own future. Don't blame your failures on others. Don't just discard the failures; use them as learning vehicles, as stepping stones to success.

The great message both the above books project, is that if you want something to happen badly enough, your attitude and positive action are going to create situations where you will succeed!

Certainly, faith can move mountains, but what positive action can you take? First, you are going to agree that you *can* and *will* influence your life, and that you can achieve the things you really want, if you work through a *life planning exercise*. Working through the exercise is itself a learning exercise.

Life planning

I wonder how many people have really had the opportunity to do this? Those who experience the 'mid-life crisis' where they question their past, and the desirability of continuing the path they tread into the future, may all have one factor in common. For those members of the population who are in their 40s or 50s, the opportunities when they left school were not good. Britain had just been at war, and the opportunity to pursue a new future was partly restricted. When these people took a job, many looked on it as a security anchor, something that was necessary to maintain a standard of living. There was little choice.

Since those times, we have seen the rise of consumerism, and experienced a substantial rise in the standard of living. Many in their 40s and 50s look back and decide that now their family is grown and away, they will do something different.

Life values

Life values are then brought into question and people have to make decisions based upon their past and their expectation for the future.

The first part in any life planning activity is to ask yourself what you would like to achieve over the next five years. Some say, 'To keep my job', 'To be secure', 'To have my health and strength'. These phrases mean nothing. What does mean something is a strong positive choice to define and go for something that is tangible and measurable.

What does security mean? A permanent full-time or part-time job? Does health mean no serious illness, or actively, physically well? Clear, precise statements are necessary. Some may argue that real life isn't like this, we can't always have what we want! Wants are fickle and not realistic. But, we can plan and make decisions now, to take the necessary steps to have what we need!

Life and career planning

Many managers, when asked what they want to achieve five years hence, gave the reply, 'More money and increased status.' But this is only one part of life. To ensure that we look at the whole life, we have to split up life into discrete but overlapping areas. Using the approach of Pedlar, Burgoyne and Boydell, it is possible, in a fairly short period of time, to work through some of the stages of life planning.

You should ask yourself what you would have hoped to achieve in such important key areas as employment, wealth, relationships and self-development.

- *Employment and your career*: The organization for which you work, the type and level of job you do, the typical tasks you perform and your responsibilities.
- *Wealth and material possessions*: The type of house in which you wish to live, your car, your life style which is reflected by the general accommodation, furniture and those things which carry status in social situations.
- *Relationships*: Here, I am not only referring to those with your wife or husband, but the positive and caring relationships you develop with your children, your parents, your brothers and sisters, etc. What sort of relationship do you wish to create with friends, colleagues, etc? Are these friendships transient or do you maintain lifetime friendships with just a few people? Be specific. ·

- *Self-development and actualization*: Are there any particular skills you wish to develop? Do you want to explore your other potentialities? Do you want to acquire new knowledge, test your attitudes and acquire new skills? Do you want to take a postgraduate management qualification? How will this affect your career and how you feel about yourself? Will your self-esteem and worth be enhanced? How will this impact upon your values and the way you think about, and live, your life?

These are all questions that you should try to answer, and when you have, think through the degree to which your objectives:

- *Complement* each other;
- *Conflict with* each other.

For instance, if you want to move further up to a senior management position, it is unlikely you will achieve your objective without some sort of management qualification. Will you need to pursue an MBA or gain corporate membership of a professional body? If you are not prepared to do this, what are your chances of success? Are they high or low in your own organization? Will you have to move to another company?

If you do decide to pursue your career interests elsewhere, what will be the expectations of others regarding your experience? You may have no choice but to pursue the management qualification! But while you are doing this, will you find the time and energy to maintain the other aspects of your life? Will you be able to enrich and develop the relationships you have with your family and your close friends?

What are your expectations regarding your personal possessions? Will you be able to maintain your present standard of living and meet your future expectations staying in the job you presently hold?

Will you be able to spend time studying for your MBA, and what will be the financial and social cost?

These are just some of the problems associated with life and career goal clarification. These issues should be considered and evaluated because they impact upon your self-worth in the long term. Knowing what you want and having a clear idea of how you are going to achieve your goals is imperative.

A year today

To start the way you want to continue, it is worth considering the goals and objectives you would like to achieve a year from now. Think over your goals. Would you like to have got started on a part-time management development course, or perhaps registered for your MBA? Is there a particular skill you would like to improve, or would you prefer to set yourself a goal which was related to your family, your relationships with your wife and children, or is the goal spiritual, or related to a hobby or leisure interest? Whatever it is, write it down now, and think over the following issues.

The first point about goal-setting is the 'reality test'. How realistic is this goal? Will you be able to achieve it with ease, or will you be constantly under pressure to maintain a steady momentum to make it a reality? If your goal is not realistic, you will find that this will destroy your self-motivation and drive.

The runner

May I give an example? A friend who runs regularly decided to complete a marathon. This was not an unrealistic goal as he was running 30–40 miles each week. His goal determined the rigour of his training programme. He had to run a long slow distance, preferably 15–18 miles in one day over the weekend, and the rest of the sessions were composed of runs covering 5–6 miles. He completed his marathon in 4 hours 10 minutes and then he got the 'running bug'. He set himself an unrealistic target of running under 3 hours (within a year), a feat only achieved by 10 per cent of people who run this event and who are normally seasoned club runners!

The training he undertook was breathtaking! He stepped up his training to 70–80 miles per week. On some occasions he went out twice a day. What was the result? His running had taken over from all his other activities. Work was pushed further and further back as a priority. He also began to suffer trivial injuries, which, because of his rapid increase in mileage, led to severe injuries. After four months training, his body gave up. He had a severe knee injury which put him out of the 'chase' for several months!

The point of this story is that the enthusiasm of this person was high, and this, rather than his ability and a sensible approach to training, guided him to set a goal that was unrealistic. This created pressure, anxiety and frustration because he could not get out to pursue his goal.

Goal setting

Whatever the goal you choose, it must be realistic. For instance, some managers decide to take up an Open University course. The biggest mistake they can make is to pursue too many options or 'credits' at once. This can lead to pressure which, in time, may halt any progress at all.

The goal that you choose must be *achievable* and *realistic*. Beyond this, it must be consistent with your lifestyle and your present abilities. For instance, you would not be advised to pursue a course in operational research if your statistical and numerical ability was poor or non-existent!

Goals and objectives that are set must be *measurable*. It would be little use setting yourself a goal such as: 'to improve my man management skills'. How could you tell when these skills had been improved, and by what degree? Is there some indicator of success? Does your competence on one day improve considerably from the previous day? Clearly not. You have to set yourself *specific* and *precise* goals.

You might set yourself the target of attending a structured course on transactional analysis. Attending and pursuing the course should provide you with an insight into your interpersonal competence and your impact on the management of people. You will gain competence through experience and role playing. The course will not supply you with all the information you want or need, but the subject is specific and will give a certain perspective. Part of training in transactional analysis will help you highlight, and appreciate, other perspectives, and other areas of study. The major point is that you have a benchmark from which you can *measure* progress.

Now that you have agreed on your goal and defined it in precise, understandable, meaningful, realistic and achievable terms, you will have to think through the steps you have to take in order to achieve your goal. This means setting sub-goals.

Step by step

You need to think about the major activities and tasks you will have to perform in order to achieve your goal. If you plan to lose weight, say ten pounds by your summer holidays, you do not expect to lose it all at once, but in graduated steps. It may be two pounds per week or a ten week loss of one pound per week. The choice is yours. The important point to note is that you have to set your sub-goals by which you can measure your progress. These intermediate steps can give you feedback on your success.

Again, the key activities and steps must be agreed and set using the same principles as above. They must be realistic, achievable, etc. You must think through the sequence of the steps. If you give little thought to the smaller steps, it shows that the reality of achieving your fianl goal must be in question.

What can inhibit me achieving my goal?

Before you finally decide to 'go for it', you have to consider the major barriers which may stop you achieving your goal. For the manager who is keen to complete a management qualification it may mean seeking funding for this course from his employers. If turned down, he must make up his mind whether the course is still of sufficient interest since he will have to finance himself.

Will the manager get from his family the support that he will need to complete the course? Will he be prepared to 'sacrifice' two evenings a week for attendance and two further evenings for additional study? Only he, the manager, can decide.

What skills do you need to achieve your goal?

Now that the 'reasonableness test' is over, you should try to assess the skills and knowledge you will require to achieve the goal. For those attending a management course this may seem obvious. They would state:

'To know and apply the content of the course to real management situations and to complete the relevant course requirements.'

This is too easy! The skills and knowledge to which I refer include the determination to continue even when you would prefer to do other things, the stamina to keep reading and making notes rather than giving in and watching television. This might be reflected by your self-drive and motivation but a thorough grounding in study skills and speed reading may be critical to your eventual performance! Your effectiveness could be improved radically by taking the time to develop these and other related techniques.

Your time management skills and priority setting will also be required. You will have to decide how much time to allocate to various subjects and you will have to make choices between spending additional time on subjects that are difficult and in which you are less interested, in preference to those things that you find of interest and relevance. The point about choosing such a goal as a management qualification is that you will have to develop balance in order to do well across a range of disciplines and subjects!

What help will you need to achieve your goal?

Staying with the example above, the manager may need help and support from his colleagues at certain times of the year so that he can spend more time studying for examinations. He could develop a rota so that at other times he could provide additional time for helping others, perhaps to deal with a backload of work.

The manager is going to need a fair bit of help and support from his boss. If the latter is not committed to the 'goals' of his subordinate, then the reality of achieving the goal will be in question.

Most of all, the manager pursuing the management qualification will need help and support from his family. Every choice has an opportunity cost. If you are busy studying, your family commitments are going to be stretched. In order to promote harmony, it is best to explore the consequences of 'what is expected of you' both from your tutors and from your family's point of view. Then it is up to you to avoid the obvious conflicts and solve any problem before it arises.

Most people think of 'help' from others in terms of expertise. This area is not usually a problem, until you start moving away from the academic expertise or a functional specialism! The help that some need is very different, i.e. support and counselling.

Take as an example a telephone conversation I received some time ago. The caller wanted to talk to me about interviewing skills. He told me that he was attending a second interview for a promotion within his company. He was expected to get the job, because he had been doing it for the last year, but had not been awarded the status and the rewards which went with the responsibility. The problem was that this chap lacked any real expertise in interviewing. His performance had always been below standard. The help he needed was concerned with how he could improve his performance in the interview. We had a few discussions and practice runs which helped him improve his performance. The major point is that this manager was aware that he possessed the skills to do the job, but he lacked the expertise to convince others that he could!

What is it in 'me' which will inhibit my achieving my goal?

The most difficult question has been left to last. At this stage I would hope that most people would be fairly honest. The most obvious answers include:

- lack of planning;
- inability to set and adhere to priorities;
- indiscipline;
- lack of drive and self-motivation;
- laziness;
- looking for distractions;
- apathy;
- procrastination;
- lack of assertion;
- lack of confidence.

These all appear so negative. All of these issues have been tackled in this book. Use it as a companion to help you through the difficult times, and keep a log of how you felt before and after you have achieved your goal. Our task is to picture how we feel when we have completed the task. Think about it. Write it down now. Express your emotions and think through the consequences.

Visions of success

When you *achieve* your goal, think of the opportunities which are now open to you; what are the tangible rewards associated with the sacrifices you have made to achieve this goal? List them. Building a strong positive image and vision will help you aim for and achieve success.

All you need to do to achieve something is plan, plan and plan again, and set yourself targets. You *can* achieve your career and life goals. All that is stopping you is the will to succeed and the framework to help structure your time so that you can use it to achieve what you really want.

Examining the positive rather than the negative side of things should help you eradicate some of those elements 'within you' which may stop you achieving your goals.

Chapter 17

Managerial effectiveness

What is it that separates the high achiever from the poor performer? What special characteristics or personality traits are possessed by those who succeed and flourish in an organization, and those who never make the short-list to promotion?

We have discussed the role of luck and opportunity in the last chapter. We have not yet referred to those other attributes, skills or expertise possessed by the 'high flyer'.

What we are interested in examining are those basic factors which separate the potential senior manager from others. Research into characteristics of leadership suggest that managers who project certain personality characteristics might be successful in particular circumstances.

Without moving into the world of personality tests, is it possible to highlight those things by which we may be able to examine the potential success story? If we can do this then perhaps there is some chance of actually being able to replicate these characteristics through the process of training and development.

Myths

Traditionally, we believe that the effective manager is one who is an expert in his field and keeps up to date with new developments. We would also expect him or her to have a detailed understanding of how the organization functions, its chief goals and objectives, the strategies currently being pursued and all the other components that suggest that the manager is aware of what happens and why, and is on top of his job.

This would suggest that he has to keep his finger on the pulse, monitor changes, and react appropriately to events in order to maintain his progress.

The effective manager

The successful manager, however, is more than just a combination of 'professional expertise' and 'organizational knowledge'. Possessing the organizational information and the necessary professionalism is a *must*, a prerequisite, but not necessarily an indicator of success. The foregoing chapters of this book have highlighted some of the skills that managers need to develop if they want to achieve their goals. Reference to these *essential* skills follows.

Achieving results through others

Successful managers have to be able to respond quickly to events. They have to make accurate decisions based upon the ideas of many other people with different shades of opinion. The decision-making forum is where the successful manager shines. He stands out from his less successful counterparts because he has a structure and the necessary social and interpersonal skills first to get others to contribute, and secondly to gain agreement. The ability to persuade and negotiate with others is a key skill.

Having faith and confidence in others and taking the time to *delegate* properly, and with care and attention, leaves the manager free to pursue more important work and provides the right training and coaching for his staff.

Meetings management

Knowing how much time a manager spends at both informal and formal meetings suggests that the man who can influence events, even though he may not occupy the role of chairman, is the man who is noticed as someone who is not just there to get the decision he wants, but there to ensure that the opinion of others is taken into account.

Emotional resilience

The rate at which 'change' is accelerating and the impact that change has upon our business lives suggest that successful and effective managers are those who are quick to adapt, and, in some circumstances, anticipate and plan for change.

Not too many people possess the emotional resilience to be able to adapt to the 'dizzying rate of change', and those who do will rise above their colleagues. Developing the ability to identify and manage your *stress* is crucial for managers who are expected to function in a number of different environments!

Problem solving

Finding innovative solutions to problems differentiates the effective manager from his colleague who refuses to try new ways of working. Being willing to take a 'calculated risk', developing new solutions to old problems and getting others to try new techniques are demonstrations of clear leadership.

Rejecting some of the old outmoded approaches to problem solving, and involving others in creative techniques, are characteristics of the manager who wants to build a cohesive team committed to the same goals as himself. The solutions, and paths to putting them into practice, may differ, but the enthusiasm and commitment to 'make things happen' will shine out and act as a beacon for others to try these new ways of working.

Managing yourself

Knowing more about yourself, and understanding the situations in which you are effective, helps you in planning for the future. Knowing how and when to respond to others, and developing, practising and becoming expert in *assertiveness* should help you to guard your time in order that you achieve your key result areas.

Taking decisive action

Thinking is an activity on which managers do not spend enough time. They prefer to act instead. This situation can be created by unfortunate circumstances within the organization which creates the firefighting mentality! If the manager can rise above this, and take decisive action when necessary, he will be viewed as a man of action.

Others in the organization may not wish to take the risk, and use *thinking* as an excuse for *procrastination*. The effective manager is the one who is aware that refusing to make a decision is just as bad as making the wrong decision. Being decisive, owning and living up to your responsibilities, is what will separate you from those who will never reach senior status.

Administrative efficiency

The successful manager does not spend all his time working through strategic issues, but also consumes vast quantities of information and paperwork. A manager who has mastered the short-term paperwork problem works on an organized desk and does not have to spend too much time firefighting. He understands that the routine steady-state functions are the foundations upon which he can build new structures and plans. He knows that without the solid foundation, his plans can be no more than ideas or flights of fantasy. He reads for results and writes to express. He does not waste needless time on administration. He develops balance.

Career and life planning

The effective manager is one who is not just absorbed in work, but one who believes that there must be balance between work and leisure. He knows what he wants and he knows how to structure his time to achieve his objectives. He plans ahead, not just one week or a month in advance, but for the long term. He has discussed his ideas with his family and ironed out any areas of conflict. He has assessed his strengths and weaknesses and is determined to build upon his previous successes.

He plans ahead for the important things in his life, and ensures that he is prepared for dealing with the big problems, because he has anticipated them. He has carefully undertaken the activity of career and life planning.

Pragmatism

Finally, the effective manager is a realist. He does not just read books for interest and intellectual pursuit, but he decides to put them into practice and innovate upon the ideas presented. He is positive and will spend time trying to make something work, rather than finding reasons to make it fail!

The effective manager is, in short, determined to make the most of his time and always ensure that not just is he . . .

'Doing the job right, but doing the right job.'

If this fails, there is always a way to ensure that he achieves results through *time management*. He asks himself a simple question.

'What is the best use of my time right now?'

Index